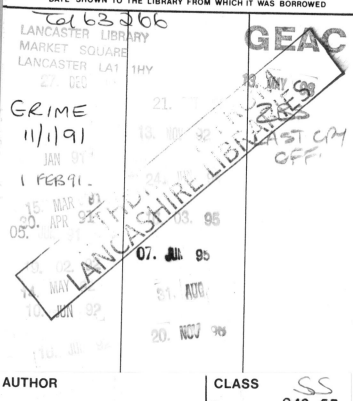

Special Relations

Compiled by Jocelyn Statler

Special Relations

Transatlantic letters linking
three English evacuees and their families, 1940–45

IMPERIAL WAR MUSEUM

Published by the Imperial War Museum, Lambeth Road, London SE1 6HZ

Copyright © Jocelyn Statler 1990
Preface © Trustees of the Imperial War Museum 1990

Dust jacket illustration by Jean-Paul Tibbles

Designed by Herbert Spencer
Printed and bound in Great Britain by Butler & Tanner Ltd, Frome, Somerset, BA11 1NF

Distributed by Octopus Distribution Services Ltd

Photographs
National Maritime Museum, Greenwich, 13
Associated Press, 15
All others Jocelyn Statler

British Library Cataloguing in Publication Data
Special relations: transatlantic letters linking three English evacuees and their families, 1940–45.
    1. United States. Evacuees. Children. Child evacuees. Social life, 1933–45. Biographies.
Collections
    I. Statler, Jocelyn *1938–*   II. Imperial War Museum
    973.09170922

ISBN 0–901627–54–2

Foreword

One of the characteristics of modern war is that it affects everyone. In past centuries war was the business of the fighting man and the civilian population was involved almost accidentally. Of course, this was of little comfort if your town or village happened to be in the path of an invading army, but given reasonable good fortune our civilian ancestors might hope to live out their lives without being touched by war. All this has changed in the twentieth century and in the age of total war special efforts have had to be made to protect children. One way of doing this was evacuation – most commonly in Britain from the town to the country, but in some 5,000 instances across the Atlantic to the safer haven of the United States.

This book tells the story of a family who sent their children to America. The lives of all involved, especially of the children, were changed for ever by this experience, but as these charming letters show the changes were on the whole beneficial. They also reveal a little known aspect of Anglo-American co-operation and remind us how much the civilian population of America did during the Second World War to help their British counterparts.

Those who read these pages may also like to be reminded that the Imperial War Museum is the largest national archive concerned with modern war and that we are always interested in acquiring personal papers, documents, and memorabilia relating to our subject. While only a few manuscripts can be published, all our holdings are available for students and scholars to use.

The publication of these letters is, as usual, the result of much work by many people. The brunt of the effort is borne by Mrs Jan Mihell and Dr Christopher Dowling, and I remain very grateful to both of them. This is the tenth title in the series of personal reminiscences published by the Imperial War Museum and both the series as a whole and this particular volume represent an achievement of which we can be justly proud.

Alan Borg, Director General September 1990
Imperial War Museum

For all my special relations

MATHEWS (One Ts)

John (1902)————Grace (1900)

Clifford (1928)   Sheila (1930)   Dinah (1934)   Jo (1938)

MATTHEWS (Two Ts)

Bill (1896)————Janet (1896)

'B' (1920)——Mary   Harry (1922)——Betty   Don (1925)

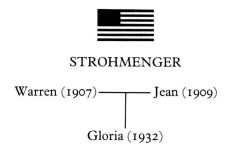

STROHMENGER

Warren (1907)————Jean (1909)

Gloria (1932)

Clifford, Dinah and Sheila Mathews in 1940.

Introduction

In the summer of 1940 my parents were living near Southampton, which was at that time a major target for German bombing raids. Following the fall of France and with the increased threat of an invasion from across the Channel they were, like all parents in the area, in constant fear for the safety of their young family. At this time they heard of a plan to send children abroad which was being sponsored by the English Speaking Union. The American head-quarters of the Union had proposed a scheme to rescue British children from the 'psychological stresses and physical danger of war' by evacuating as many as possible to the USA. The programme was being organised in London by the American Committee for the Evacuation of Children and operated in America under the auspices of the United States Committee for the Care of European Children.

After much anguished weighing of the pros and cons, my parents decided that the situation at home made the separation and the dangers of the journey worthwhile, and they embarked on the process of registration and getting together the necessary clothes and the money for the passage, no small undertaking as they were not wealthy people. The three oldest children were to go: John Clifford, twelve years old, Sheila ten and Dinah five. The fourth, still not two years old, was too young to be sent.

My father's strong belief in the basic goodness of human nature and the hope that the war would not last long gave my parents the courage to take part in the venture, for they had no idea where in the USA the children would go, or with whom they would be living.

The scheme presented its organisers with enormous difficulties, which had to be overcome, in terms of American immigration laws, organising transport and finding homes for the children, as well as supervising their welfare once they were settled. Only American optimism, determination that the ends could be achieved, efficiency and the tremendous hard work of those running the programme made the success of such an undertaking possible in the conditions of wartime Britain.

The American Committee, operating from Grosvenor House, Park Lane, London, managed to send nearly 1,000 children to the USA, according to English Speaking Union records, before its activities were suspended in November 1940. A parallel scheme, which the British government was organising for children whose parents could not afford the fare, was suspended in August 1940. At the time, after the collapse of France, it was said that the Royal Navy could no longer spare ships to escort the passenger liners. It was also said that the government was alarmed at the huge number of applications it was receiving.

The need for escort ships was very real, however. My parents were horrified shortly after they had sent off their trio with no information as to which ship they were on, to see a picture in their newspaper which showed a little girl, who looked at first sight very like Sheila, wrapped in a blanket, having been rescued from the sea after the sinking of the *City of Benares*. This liner, torpedoed by the Germans, had 98 British children on board, of whom only 13 survived. Fortunately their own children were on the RMS *Antonia*, the last such evacuee ship to be allowed to sail for the USA, and they had a safe crossing.

My parents waited in suspense from mid-September, when the children left, until late November to know where and with whom they were staying in the USA. At last, to their great relief, they heard that Cliff was staying with Janet and Bill Matthews (who, by coincidence, had the same surname but spelled with two Ts, so that the families came to refer to each other as the 'One Ts' and the 'Two Ts') and the girls with Jean and Warren Strohmenger in villages in Ohio not far apart. It is not difficult to imagine how important the first letters were, bringing the news from the States, how carefully preserved and passed round all the branches of the family who wanted to know how the children were getting on. We do have to remind ourselves how little ordinary British people knew then about life in the USA before the age of TV and mass tourist travel. No wonder that details of everyday life were pleaded for in the correspondence which developed between those involved. As a result the letters provide an intimate glimpse of family life on both sides of the Atlantic during the war, not as it might be remembered, but as it was at the time.

No wonder also that for personal reasons the letters were preserved, though my father from the first felt that they would contain the story of an interesting experiment in human and international relations which should be told at some later date. He believed his children had a job to do as ambassadors for Britain in the USA, as they would later when they returned, for the USA in Britain – a mighty burden for the shoulders of children not yet in their teens. However, as an American magazine observed at the time, 'If the movement from Britain becomes a mass evacuation, one of the fondest dreams of sociologists will be realised ... A future generation of English will feel a lot warmer towards Americans, and vice versa, than if they had never met.' I do not believe a major sociological study of the broader effects of the scheme has yet been undertaken, but its effect on my own family has been fundamental.

As the reader may now have deduced, I am the youngest of the family, Jo, who stayed in England. I had known of the letters, though I could not read them at the time, of course, and I was delighted to rediscover them when helping my mother to clear her attic during a recent move of house. They were of special interest to me because they explained so much of the background which has made my family what it is now and the influences which have shaped us. However, I soon began to agree with my father's original thought that they could be of wider interest. The letters give a very personal insight into the way in which the families concerned lived and reacted in trying times. They were ordinary people in special circumstances, challenged to think more explicitly than they normally would have about their attitudes to life and the bringing up of children, and not only to think, but to put their thoughts down on paper. The difficulties they were living through brought to light the unusual talent of the American foster mother, Janet Matthews, in understanding and bringing out the best in the children under her care. A record of her qualities – no heroine, she readily admitted her own faults – is worth reading in its own right, I think.

During the long evenings of blackout, when it was almost impossible to go out, my father's correspondence developed from the formal rather stilted style of the early letters to a more frank and open revelation of thoughts and fears, readily responded to on the American side. Some long distance kidding and family jokes soon crept in, for anything which raised a smile in those days was highly valued.

Fortunately for me, many of the original letters survived from both sides of the Atlantic. My father typed all of his and kept the carbon copies, though the quality of the paper and the carbon paper was so poor that some are now scarcely legible. Many of the letters had to be omitted, particularly those from the children, but from among the seven hundred which survived I tried to choose just enough to give that part of the story of my family's wartime experience, in the words of those who lived through it, which would be of most interest to other readers without needing any added commentary. However, I have written a postscript for those who may wish to have the story brought up to date.

In the task of cutting the text down to a size for publication from the letters available to me, I benefited greatly from the expert advice of Christopher Dowling, Keeper of the Department of Museum Services at the Imperial War Museum. His assistance and the work of all his staff have been instrumental in transforming an overweight manuscript into a book which I hope will be a pleasure to read and a record worth preserving.

Jocelyn Statler
April 1990

Dear Mummy and Daddy,   Liverpool
                                                Tuesday.
                           arrived here safely
yesterday, at about 4.30 in an air-raid.
We are "billeted" at a school, for a few days
before we sail. We had 5 raids last night.
The school has beautiful grounds of it's own and
we can all play. Dinah and Sheilah are very
happy. I have been playing foot-ball. I have
chummed up with a boy named Brian and Sheila
with his sister Jill. Sheila and Dinah
send their love.   Love Cliff

The first news from the Mathews children: Clifford's postcard from Liverpool on 17 September 1940.

Clifford Mathews to his parents

17 September 1940   Liverpool

Arrived here safely yesterday at about 4.30 in an air raid. We are
billeted at a school for a few days before we sail. We had five raids
last night. The school has beautiful grounds of its own and we can
all play. Dinah and Sheila are very happy. I have been playing
football. Have chummed up with a boy named Brian and Sheila with
his sister Jill. Sheila and Dinah send their love.

Clifford Mathews to his parents

September 1940   RMS *Antonia*

I hope you are keeping well and are not bothered by too many air
raids. I wonder if Jo misses us. Sheila and Dinah are very good and
are happy in their two-berth cabin. I sleep in the next cabin with
another boy. The food is excellent and the children are very nice.
We have palled up with all our section.

I am writing this as we go through the Straits of Belle Isle. We
have seen two icebergs and sailed within a hundred yards of one.

We have had bad weather so far although it is calmer today. Out
of the 120 going a hundred have been seasick. I haven't yet.

I am writing this as we go through the Straits of Belle Isle. We
have seen two icebergs and sailed within a hundred yards of one.

RMS *Antonia*.

We have been lectured on the 'Fleet Air Arm', 'Submarines', 'Convoys' and the 'Merchant Navy'. We also have a cinema every afternoon which we all enjoy.

When we were staying at the school in Liverpool we had a near escape. We had an air raid warning at about one o'clock in the morning and we all trooped down to the shelter. Suddenly we heard a whistle and four very loud explosions. Next morning no breakfast arrived: the school kitchen had been hit. A house about 30 yards along the road was also demolished.

We shall soon be landing so will write again later.

Clifford Mathews to his parents

2 October 1940   Edwin Gould Foundation, New York City

After the last letter I wrote, we continued right the way down the St Lawrence River until we came to Quebec. It was dark when we left but we were allowed to stay on deck as a special treat. It was a wonderful sight to see all the tiny lights flickering on and off, it almost seemed impossible after the blackout.

Finally we arrived at Montreal where we were billeted at a school and taught by some Canadian scouts how to play baseball. Personally I think it is tripe – more like a girl's game of rounders than anything else. Anyhow we left there in the morning and went to a beautiful station and boarded the train for New York. The train travelled twice as fast as the British but they're not so comfortable. At lunch we were given a super lunch box each and we had tea in the lovely dining salon of the train. We arrived at the Edwin Gould Foundation at about 8.30 pm and immediately were shown our beds. We have to look after and clean the whole cottage. I do the washing up after every meal and I might tell you that with three helpers it is some job.

Yesterday Mr Stuart took myself and two other boys into New York to visit some newspapers. I have had my photo taken twelve times and have been interviewed by a *Journal American* reporter. However, they evidently don't like my face for only my interview has been published.

I do not see Sheila and Dinah a lot but I am sure they are happy. We have been invited to the New York World's Fair.

Lots of love to Jo and all at home.

British evacuees arriving in New York by rail from Montreal, 1940.

Clifford Mathews to his parents

October 1940   Trelawny, Glendale, Ohio

I hope you are keeping well and are not bothered by the air raids
now. I am so sorry I have not written before but I have not had time
to since I left the Bronx Institute.

We left the institute one evening and boarded the train for Cincinnati. We slept in the train that night and the next morning we
arrived at Cincinnati at 8.30. We then went to another children's
home where we stayed the night. The next afternoon we came to
Glendale, or at least I did because Sheila and Dinah are living in the
next town about two miles away. I went to their home where they
are to stay. The lady was very nice and she has a daughter who is
about seven years old who Sheila and Dinah may play with.

I am living with Mr and Mrs Matthews who are very nice people
and I am very happy with them. Their son Don, who is about fifteen,
is also very nice and I get along very well with him. They have a
lovely big house which stands back in its own grounds from the

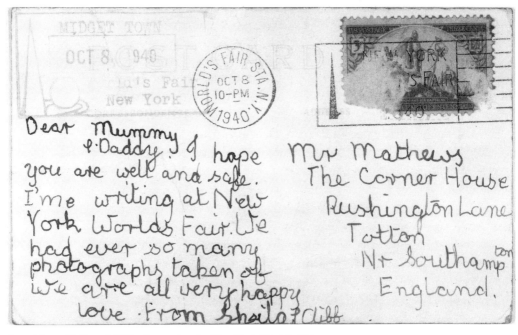

1961, Stillwell Ave
New York City
Oct. 7th 1940

Dear Mummy and Daddy,
I hope you are all as well
as I am and not having too many air-raids.
Since I wrote to you last Monday we have moved
from C cottage to F. I have had liver blood
tests and two injections. One against Tuberculosis and
the other against Scarlet Fever. Sheila and Dinah have
also had them. As well as these we have also
had a thorough medical examination.
I am writing to you now in school, as
we are given time to write a letter once a week.
We have to get up here in the morning
at 7·0 a.m. and have breakfast at 7·30 a.m., school
is at 9·0 a.m. We have lunch at 12·0 a.m. and

Part of a letter from Clifford Mathews written in New York, October 1940.

Dear Mummy
& Daddy, I hope
you are well and safe.
I'me writing at New
York Worlds Fair. We
had ever so many
photographs taken of
we are all very happy
love from Sheila & Cliff

Mr Mathews
The Corner House
Rushington Lane
Totton
Nr Southampton
England.

A card from Sheila and Clifford posted at the New York World's Fair.

main highway. They have two cocker spaniels and Sheila and Dinah fell in love with them when they saw them the other day.

The school is just across the road and I went to school yesterday just to get acquainted with the boys. They are all very nice.

The playing field is just at the back of the grounds and yesterday I went to watch a football match; it certainly is rough.

Give my love to all at home especially Jo and tell them all I shall write to them as soon as I get time.

Jean Strohmenger to Grace and John Mathews

30 October 1940   54 Forest Avenue, Wyoming, Ohio

We are very happy that Dinah and Sheila arrived at our home today at 4 pm. Clifford is staying with a family whom we know in the village adjoining ours, so they will see each other frequently. They are all very sweet children.

Dinah and Sheila seem a little thin and tired, but we hope that now they are settled down they will fatten up a little. Dinah ate every bit of her dinner and Sheila ate everything but the turnips. (Beef roast, peas, turnips, fruit salad and apple or custard pie and milk.)

Sheila and I have been busy this evening unpacking their bags and getting things put away. They are both in bed now in the double bed in the same room with Gloria, our little girl. Gloria is seven and in the second grade. They seem to be quite pleased with each other.

We will start Sheila and Dinah off to school on Monday. We think they need a day or two at home to get used to us. Friday is a holiday anyway (annual teachers' meeting) and our children don't go to school on Saturday. We'll start Sheila in Gloria's piano class and also start them both in the horseback riding class with Gloria. We all like to ride and the girls said they would enjoy it. They were out playing with the children in the neighborhood this afternoon, laughing and having a big time, and I believe they are going to like it here.

I know you are curious about us, so I'll state a few facts and then you'll know a little, anyway. I'll also enclose some snapshots. We hope to take some pictures of the girls tomorrow or the next day, and I'll send them soon. First I'll tell you about Doctor. Warren is a physician, thirty-three years old. He graduated from medical school in June 1931 and we were married then at Louisville,

17

SHEILA, DINAH AND JOHN MATHEWS

English children who are temporarily at the Children's Home while being assigned to foster homes in this country for the "duration" are pictured.

Left, left to right, are Sheila Betty Mathews, 10, her sister, Angela Dinah, 5, and their brother, John, 12.

Sheila, Dinah and Clifford in Cincinnati.
(*Cincinnati Times–Star*, 31 October 1940).

Opposite: Jean Strohmenger's first letter to John and Grace Mathews.

Kentucky, my home. He interned for a year in a hospital in Cincinnati (we live 12 miles out from town) and then he started in general practice. He has a very nice practice. He has a ten-room office about a mile away from our home. And, oh yes, in case you are afraid from the German name that your children have jumped from the frying pan into the fire, his grandparents on his father's side came from Germany and he and his father are both very much disgusted with Hitler and the rest of the German and Italian outfits. Doctor's mother is American from way back, of Welsh, Scotch-Irish and Dutch extraction.

I am thirty-one years old, college educated, and keep busy at home with a few outside duties. I work with the Women's Auxiliary at the Episcopal Church, I'm secretary of the City Council of Girl Scouts and I'm secretary of the Children's Hospital Cooperative Board. My mother was born in Stirling, Scotland, and my father in Londonderry, Ireland. (They live in Louisville.)

We built our home five and a half years ago in a nice residential suburb. We have a negro maid, in whom the girls are quite interested. Warren's mother and father have an apartment on the second floor. We live in a one-family house, but they have their own living room, bedroom, kitchen and bathroom. We have four rooms on the first floor and have two bedrooms and bathroom on the third floor.

I'll try to write you about once a week and the girls want to write, but I'll send this by Clipper so you'll know they are settled, & safe.

MRS. WARREN STROHMENGER
54 FOREST AVENUE
WYOMING, OHIO

Thursday, Oct 30, '40

Dear Mr & Mrs Mathews

We are very happy that Dinah and Shelia arrived at our home today at 4:00 P.M. Clifford is staying with a family whom we know in the village adjoining ours, so they will see each other frequently. They are all very sweet children.

Dinah and Shelia seem a little thin and tired, but we hope that

Nov. 1st

Dear Mrs. Matthews,

Many months ago we asked to have your little English boy's visit us for the "duration". Nothing happened and we gave up hope. Then, last Wednesday we were suddenly told about Clifford and we were delighted. As my fifteen year old son said "If we had had a chance to choose a child from all the children who have ever was, we couldn't have found a nicer boy." He is indeed a most beguiling little fellow and we are grateful to you for sending him to us—

No doubt you would like to know something about us. My husband and I are forty-four years old. We were married during the last war and my husband served in France with the American army. We have three boys—one twenty, one eighteen and one

Janet Matthews's first letter to John and Grace Mathews.

We think you made a very wise move in sending the girls and boy to America. I can assure you they will be well cared for. There have only been five children sent to the Cincinnati area, your three and twin boys.

I will try to write you about once a week and the girls want to write, but I'll send this by clipper so you'll know they are settled and safe.

Janet Matthews to Grace Mathews

1 November 1940   Trelawny, Glendale, Ohio

Many months ago we asked to have some little English boys visit us for the 'duration'. Nothing happened and we gave up hope. Then, on Wednesday, we were suddenly told about Clifford and we were delighted. As my fifteen-year-old son said, 'If we had had a choice from all the children who have come over, we couldn't have found a nicer boy.' He is a most beguiling little fellow and we are grateful to you for lending him to us.

No doubt you would like to know something about us. My husband and I are forty-four years old. We were married during the last war and my husband served in France with the American army. We have three boys, 'B' who is twenty, Harry who is eighteen and Don who is fifteen. The two older boys are away at college and the youngest boy is at home. All our boys are fond of younger children and will be brotherly in their attitude toward Clifford, I feel sure.

We live thirteen miles outside of Cincinnati, Ohio, in a little village called Glendale. It is a residential district with a population slightly over two thousand. Our house is a little on the biggish side, but it is not at all formal. We have always enjoyed having the boys' friends here and we allow dogs to sit in the chairs, so there is no need for the children to worry about taking care of the furniture.

There is an excellent public school a short walk from the house and all of our children have attended it. Clifford and I went over and talked about his studies and on Monday he will start at school.

There are a number of twelve-year-old boys in the village and we have already made contacts with them and our athletic director, so I think we should have no trouble with recreation. There is also quite a good library at school and our boys have always enjoyed it as I'm sure your boy will.

We have an excellent music department and if Clifford is interested he will have an opportunity to attend symphony concerts and play any instrument he might choose.

I have made us sound quite dull, but we really are a rather noisy and hilarious family at times. We spend a lot of time with our boys and they seem to enjoy having talks with their father and playing tennis with their mother and we frequently go to Cincinnati together for a movie.

Sometimes I think we have not brought our children up well and sometimes they are so fine I almost burst with pride. We will attempt to be wise with your boy and profit by our mistakes with our own children. At least you will know that he is with people who love and understand boys. We talk about you and his father and will attempt to follow any suggestions you would like to make.

Sheila and Dinah are not far away. The children can be together as much as they like. I know Mrs Strohmenger and she is a delightful young person – I am sure the little girls will be happy with her.

I promise *never* to talk about us in any future letters but I know you must be curious. One last thing, we are happily married and there will be no bickering to distress a small boy.

We, in America, look with awe upon the courage of the British and it is a great pleasure to do a tiny bit for our small English boy. I really think he is as happy as is possible so far from home and with strange people. We will do everything in our power to keep him well and happy.

Jean Strohmenger to Grace and John Mathews

4 November 1940   54 Forest Avenue, Wyoming, Ohio

I have the girls in bed now and things are quiet, so I'll start a letter to you, although I probably won't mail it until the end of the week when they can write their little notes.

I believe the girls are settling down and getting used to us and the country very well. Of course, the fact that we speak with a different accent and use other words to describe things makes it a little hard for them, but they are gradually getting used to it. They are behaving beautifully. Our main difficulty is with our own child. She has always been alone and now with two new children she has gone wild. Since they came to our house Wednesday afternoon they have been on the go all the time.

Thursday we went shopping and got new heavy winter outfits with snow pants. Sheila mentioned you might send winter clothes. Don't do that. Give any you have to children in England. Here in America we wear lightweight clothes in the house but very heavy clothes outside. We have basements in our homes with furnaces that warm all the rooms. We got Sheila a new velvet party dress and a skirt and two blouses. Two friends of ours have given her lovely dresses and I had a lot of things for Dinah that Gloria had outgrown. Gloria has a very indulgent grandmother who gives her more dresses than she can wear.

Friday afternoon Clifford and Mrs Matthews came to see us, as did the Minister. They will all go to Sunday school at the Episcopal church where Gloria goes.

Today was their first day at school. They tell me their English school was not as large. I believe there are almost 900 children in this school. Dinah shed some tears when I took her into class this morning but we walked up and down the hall a few times and she got over it.

The school and the neighbourhood have taken in the girls with open arms and it is touching the sweet things that are done for them. The very day they came the children were all waiting around for

The Strohmenger's house, 54 Forest Avenue, Wyoming, Ohio.

them to arrive, and before very many minutes Sheila was riding Gordon's new bicycle and the little girls were holding Dinah on a small two-wheeler. It would do your hearts good to see them playing and racing around.

Just yesterday I calmed down and got over the fright I had over taking two girls instead of one. You see, last June we wrote and asked to take a little girl between one and five years for the duration of the war. Ever since, we have been filling in forms and entertaining investigators from the children's home. We had given up all hope of any children getting here, however, and then out of a clear sky the investigator from the home called and asked if we would take two girls instead of one. She said they were sisters and the home didn't think they should be separated.

We were in a quandary. There are at least eighty families here in Cincinnati who have asked for children and I couldn't understand why they wanted us to take two. Anyway, we went over to the home and saw the girls and then I could understand why they didn't want to separate them, but I still wondered why they had us first on the list when most of the other families had more money and staffs of servants. That was cleared up for me too. I think you would appreciate the care the children's home is using in placing them. They realise that the children will all be going back to their homes in England and they don't want them getting used to servants if they won't have them when they go home. Also they wanted to put the children with younger folks and with a child. We had the girls the very next afternoon, so you see I didn't have much time to get ready.

When the girls asked me what they should call us I suggested that since we were Gloria's mother and daddy and as she was willing to share us with them that they could call us their American mother and daddy. I hope you won't mind.

I will close for tonight. Doctor will be home from evening office hours pretty soon, and since we're both tired we'll go to bed.

Clifford Mathews to his parents

November 1940   Trelawny, Glendale, Ohio

I got my first letter from you this morning and I was so pleased because I had begun to worry. As soon as I had finished school this afternoon Mrs Matthews drove me to Wyoming to show it to Sheila

and Dinah. They were so excited. They are getting along fine. Sheila has started her music and they are both horse riding.

I am a Boy Scout now and I am studying hard to pass the Tenderfoot Test so that I can get my uniform.

Two of my friends, Tommy Jacobs and Davy Peck, and I have joined together and have made an aeroplane club. We buy the kits and make the planes and then sell them with about 20 cents profit. We are now in the middle of one with a 7-foot wingspan. It really is a terrific size. I wish you could see it. Mr Jacobs has promised us a gasoline engine for it when it is finished. We have five orders for planes to be finished before Christmas, so we shall have to work hard.

I noticed you have mentioned about our money. We have not received it yet because it has been mislaid somewhere, but the American Committee has assured me that if it has been lost or stolen they will refund it for us. So don't worry.

From your letter I should say there was quite a bit of excitement when those two German planes came down low and used their machine guns. I always miss the exciting bits.

Well, now I had better begin my homework. It's the only thing that makes life unhappy here.

Send my best wishes to all at home.

Janet Matthews to Grace Mathews

15 November 1940   Trelawny, Glendale, Ohio

Cliff and the girls were thrilled with their first letters from home. They all look rested and their color is much better than when they arrived, tired after their long trip.

The teachers at school speak enthusiastically of Cliff's attractive personality and bright mind. He seems to have a lot of friends among the boys and is very proud of his ability to play American games.

He amused us last night by saying that he was picking up American slang so fast that he didn't talk like an Englishman at all. My husband told him that he was just being polite and trying not to be different, and that when he went back to England he would soon forget our speech.

Our two older boys come home from college for three days at the end of this month. I have sent them newspaper pictures of Clifford

Janet and Bill Matthews on holiday.
Janet enclosed this photograph in her first letter to England.

Harry, 'B' and Don Matthews at their home in Glendale, Ohio.

Sheila and Dinah wearing their new coats,
outside the Strohmengers' house with Gloria,
3 November 1940.

Sheila and Dinah Mathews, ready for
Sunday School in new velvet frocks, with
Gloria Strohmenger, 3 November 1940.

and they are anxious to see him. I think he will enjoy the boys – they are full of fun and make the house seem very gay while they are here. Don is very fond of Cliff and they get along beautifully – not a cross word so far – and it is fun to see them romping together on the lawn. Don is big for his age and he looks like a St Bernard playing with a puppy.

School work is different here, but Cliff has no difficulty adjusting to it. The superintendent intends to keep your little boy busy without overtaxing him and is watching his progress with interest.

We think of you often and hope that all is well. The world is such a mess that it is hard to visualise anything in the future but we do all look forward to the ultimate success of the British. I hope it will all be over soon and that you will have your darling children with you again. Meanwhile we do our best.

American Committee for the Evacuation of Children to Grace and John Mathews

18 November 1940

American Express, 6 Haymarket,
London SW1

We wish to thank you very much for your letter of the 13th instant and are very glad to hear that you are so satisfied with the manner in which your children's evacuation to the USA has been carried out.

We are sorry to learn that you have not yet been notified of the final destination of the children and we trust that you will soon be advised of their address . . .

John and Grace Mathews to Janet and Bill Matthews

26 November 1940

The Corner House, Rushington Lane,
Totton, Hampshire

We received your letter today and as there has been delay in delivery, probably due to censorship, I am replying by air mail so that you may know as soon as possible that we have received the good news.

When my wife and I decided to send the children to America we had no idea where they would go or to whom they would be sent. Almost the only contacts we had had with Americans were with the men and women of the American Committee at Grosvenor House, London. Those contacts however gave us the impression that if they were any criterion of the treatment our children would receive in the USA then we could be quite happy about sending them. Your letter has completely confirmed that impression.

If Cliff were asked to describe your letter he would say it was 'super' (a favourite expression of his) but personally I am at a loss to convey to you in words how thankful and delighted my wife and I were after reading it. How thankful we were, too, that Cliff has been so extremely fortunate as to arrive in a happy family circle such as yours obviously is. We imagined all sorts of things happening to him, but we never in our dreams hoped for anything better. He must be thrilled to bits.

Your boys must be just as proud of you as you are of them judging by your holiday snap, and looking at Mr Matthews is it any wonder that we were able to defeat the Huns so quickly in 1918? We are happy to know that he returned to you safe and apparently well. The boys look a fine trio and no doubt hope one day to each be as good as his father. It was a grand idea sending the photographs and we thank you for them.

My wife should of course be writing this letter, but she says that all she can think of is 'I thank you', 'I thank you', 'I thank you', and although that may be expressive she agrees it is not quite enough in the circumstances. There is an air raid warning on at the moment too, and that makes it rather difficult to concentrate. Therefore she has delegated the job to me on the understanding that she writes to you in the near future. So will you excuse her?

You mention in your letter that you will endeavour to profit by the mistakes you have made in bringing up your own children, and that in dealing with Cliff you will attempt to follow any suggestions we have to make. Your letter and the fact that your boys are happy with you tells us all we wish to know. We should not presume to make any suggestions whatever. We would ask rather that you favour us by forgetting the idea of 'profiting by mistakes' and that you deal with Cliff as you would your own son. Let him rough it a little whenever possible. You see, we don't believe in coddling a boy. We think a boy should learn as soon as possible to be independent, to stand on his 'own two legs' as it were, and you probably think the same. I cannot remember ever thrashing Cliff, our idea being that he would come to us with his troubles and we could then explain to him where he had gone wrong, whereas if he was thrashed he probably would not come back again and we should then have to discover his faults in a roundabout way. In short we just wanted him to grow up dead straight and truthful. His one big fault is that he is inclined to be a little 'bossy', he likes to be the Big White Chief. He probably gets that from his father anyway.

You have promised never to talk about yourselves again in future letters. *Please* break that promise in your very next letter because we are frightfully interested and want to know all about you.

What an extraordinary coincidence that your name should be so similar to our own.

It was good of you to tell us so much about yourselves. What can I tell you about us in return? Cliff knows the family history and will no doubt talk to you about us. My wife and I are thirty-eight and forty years old respectively. We began to notice each other when we were fourteen years old. We became *really* serious at fifteen and almost began saving our pennies to get married when we were sixteen. I went off to China and Japan when I was seventeen, made a little money, and when I was twenty came back and started poultry farming. It was a bad mistake and I then had to make a fresh start, but we managed to get married in '26. I won't bore you with any more of that.

We have received a very nice letter from Mrs Strohmenger, and here again we are very fortunate, especially as you are acquainted and the children will be able to meet occasionally.

Perhaps you would like to know a little of what is happening over here. I see in the news this evening that Mr Kennedy,[1] speaking in Hollywood, stated that the British have 'virtually lost the war'. A few minutes after that the radio announcer stated that the British fleet were chasing the Italian navy up the Mediterranean. No, we have not lost the war yet, so please don't let Mr Kennedy mislead you. Actually of course we have not yet really got going, but when with the wonderful assistance your country is giving us we have attained something like parity in the air, then Hitler will begin to wish that he had not pushed us into this ghastly business.

I am enclosing a few cuttings reporting a raid which took place last Saturday on our home town.[2] As you may guess, 250 tons of

[1] Joseph Patrick Kennedy, 1888–1969. Ambassador to London, 1937–1941. Father of President John F Kennedy. To Churchill's concern, he made no secret of his doubts about Britain's staying power.
[2] Southampton suffered its first major raid on 23 November 1940. The following weekend the city centre was devastated in an even heavier attack (referred to in later letters) in which 137 people were killed and 471 seriously injured.

bombs dropping in one night is not exactly a pleasant experience, but the next morning people were carrying on much the same, except of course those who were shocked or homeless. Naturally each such raid means quite a number of killed and injured. Personally I feel that no amount of that sort of thing will win the war for Hitler. Whether the Huns can take the same medicine remains to be seen. We hope to give them some anyway. A few days ago two German bombers dived out of the clouds over our house and commenced machine gunning everyone they could see, including women and children in the local recreation ground. We simply do not understand that sort of brutality, or the fanatical hatred which will allow their submarine crews to ward off with boathooks swimming survivors of one of our vessels. Before this war commenced I believe the majority of people in this country were only too willing to be friendly with the Germans, and a great number of British tourists visited their country every year. But their actions since September '39 have effectively destroyed any desire for friendship for probably a century to come.

Cliff may have told you that my two brothers are in the fighting services, and I am enclosing 'snaps' taken during the last Fleet Review showing my wife and I with my elder brother.[1] My younger brother Tom is in the air force.[2] They would not accept me as they say I am more use to them in my present job with the Petroleum Board.[3]

Well, I think it about time I ended this lengthy epistle. By the way, I am not sure that the censor will pass the cuttings, but I see no reason why he should not. When you are good enough to write us again don't hesitate to ask as many questions as you like on any subject of interest to you and I will do my best to answer them.

---

[1] Henry Leonard Mathews, born 1899.
[2] Thomas Jesse Mathews, born 1911.
[3] A body set up at the beginning of the war with the aim of achieving maximum efficiency in the distribution of petrol and oil.

DEAR MUMMY
AND DADDY
GLORIA AND I
WEN CHRISTMAS
SHOPPING. SHEILA
WENT WITH
DADDY.
LOVE FROM
DINAH XXXXXXX XXXXX
JOSIE XXXX

A letter from Dinah, 10 December 1940.

Janet Matthews to Grace Mathews

4 December 1940   Trelawny, Glendale, Ohio

Your cable came this noon while Clifford was having his luncheon and caused great rejoicing in our household. I heard the cook calling down to the laundress, 'Wonderful news. Clifford's family are safe.' We have been very anxious about you and it was very kind of you to let us know that all is well. My husband first heard of the serious

Clifford in the drive at Trelawny.

raid while riding in his car and hurried home to be with Clifford
when he listened to the late afternoon news from London. They
talked of the destruction and the comparatively small loss of life and,
while the child was naturally disturbed, I think he was somewhat
comforted. He is such a brave little soldier! We try to avoid talk of
the war and its horrors, but it is difficult to eliminate it completely
for it is uppermost in everyone's mind.

Our two older boys were here last week and the house was full of
noise and laughter. They were instantly drawn to Cliff and he seemed
to find them highly amusing. They had a great time playing with a
football on the lawn. Mr Matthews had seen a candid camera shot
of himself recently which made him decide that he needed reducing
so he joined in. He is a bit stiff as a result and no thinner as far as I
can see.

Once a year in Glendale the parents put on a musical comedy.

The orchestra is mostly parents and most of the music is original. From the proceeds, a gift is given to our school – usually about $700. We are in the midst of this ordeal right now. We haven't taken Cliff to any of the rehearsals, but I have a seat in the front row for him for the performance.

My husband is playing the bass fiddle in the orchestra and our Donald plays the drums. I am in a dance chorus, so Cliff will feel that his American family is well represented. The proceeds this year go to 'Bundles for Britain'[1] and there is a very pro-British flavor to the whole thing.

We do not see Sheila and Dinah as much as we would if it was not winter. The girls have had slight colds and we have kept away to avoid catching them, but Clifford chats with them frequently by telephone and they seem quite happy and are doing excellent work at school.

You may be sure that our thoughts are often with you, hoping that you are keeping safe and well. We are a poor substitute for real parents but we are doing our best to make your boy's American contacts wholesome and happy. We all think that we have the very best little Englishman right here at our house and we hope some day to meet his parents and Jo.

John Mathews to Jean and Warren Strohmenger

14 December 1940   Michelmersh, near Romsey, Hampshire

I very much regret only having written you such a short note recently but everything has been in absolute turmoil. It is not a lot better now, but I feel I must break away from business and write you a reasonable letter.

In the first place, will you please excuse my always typing my letters – handwriting is purgatory to me. Also you may look askance at the paper and envelopes we use but one has to grab whatever is going nowadays. However, I am sure you will understand in these abnormal times.

We received a letter from you today which appears to be the first that you wrote after the children arrived. It is dated 30 October and

---

[1] A voluntary organisation established on 30 December 1939 which gathered and shipped blankets and clothes to bombed-out British families. It also provided medical supplies, mobile canteens and cash donations. By the end of 1940 there were some five hundred branches in forty-six states.

should have come by air. I do not have your more recent letter with me and, by the way, that is another thing which I hope you will not object to. Everyone wants to read the letters, and yours, the ones from the children and from Mrs Matthews are all somewhere in London travelling between my aunts and uncles. This is at my mother's request. My colleagues at business also want to read your letters. This is a bit thick, I know, but you must not mind because you see everyone is so interested and keen to know what you American people are like, as we in turn are only too happy to show them in order to prove that what we say about you is true. I cannot tell you how grateful we are to you because it is one of those things words simply cannot express. We can only hope that one day we may be able to make some practical demonstration of our gratitude. Sheila and Dinah are too young to realise just how fortunate they are. We just pray they will repay you by being as good as young children of their age possibly can be.

Now to answer some of your questions. We think it was a great idea having the children address you as Mummy and Daddy, especially as we could hope for nothing better than that you should be just that to them for the duration. You mention that they were both looking a little thin. I expect you will find them difficult to fatten because we are a thin family. I have never weighed more than 160 lb although I am 5 feet 11½ inches in height.

We are glad to know that the girls have taken to Gloria. Sheila especially is good at getting on with other girls, or boys for that matter. She used to be a little mother to Dinah over here and I've no doubt she will be a help to you in that way. Dinah loves a game once she gets over her shyness, and I expect by this time she and Gloria have great fun together. We would give a great deal to be able to see and hear them playing with the children in the neighbourhood. I can imagine Dinah's deep laugh bubbling over when she talks to Sheila of things which puzzle her.

Talking of her laughter reminds me of the day she went away. We nearly stopped her going, and it was only the thought of what might be in store for them that held us back. When they were leaving Grosvenor House, London, both Cliff and Sheila managed a smile for us, but as the escort, holding Dinah's hand, led her from the ballroom, tears were rolling down her face as she turned and waved her hand to us. That was a ghastly moment, believe me. However, children soon recover and we feel all right about it now that we know that she is happy again.

As you say, your name did strike us as having at least a Germanic origin, but then we always looked upon America as being somewhat cosmopolitan and therefore we quite expected that Dr Strohmenger's ancestors might have arrived in America, if not in the *Mayflower* at least many many years ago, as apparently they did. Personally, although I have been to many countries, I have never visited Germany, but friends of ours who have spent holidays there have always said what a good time they have had. The trouble has been that Hitler has imbued the youth of Germany with ideals which could only be attained by the most inhumane methods used in any war in history. I have a sneaking idea that a lot of our troubles would never occur if we spoke the same language. For example, when Chamberlain went to Munich neither he nor Hitler could speak the other's language, neither could take due note of the inflections of

Christmas 1940. Dinah and Sheila with Gloria Strohmenger.

the other's voice which can sometimes mean so much. In your country many nationalities speaking the same language seem to be able to get along quite amicably.

The reason I was only able to write you a short note in reply to your previous letter was because of a particularly heavy blitz which the Huns carried out in this vicinity. I hope you received my cable. We came through it all right, but a number of our friends lost their houses and some of them came to us for temporary shelter. As a result our house is full of refugees, and my wife and I with Jo have taken a tiny bungalow at the address on this letter. The German communiqué stated that 570 tons of bombs were dropped on Southampton. It certainly was pretty hectic while it lasted. They gave us two nights of blitz which I hope never to witness again. Of course, we get them over every night and the searchlights are always trying to pick them out. As I write this letter they are flying overhead, probably making for some town in the Midlands. The anti-aircraft batteries are firing, and so we go on. The blitz made it impossible for us to get the children Xmas presents and with all the confusion we had to give up the idea of getting anything to them on time. We have now been able to go to another town and get something, but of course thousands of others have done the same so one has to take whatever one can find. Let's hope that what we are sending arrives safely.

I am being transferred to Chichester in Sussex – the neighbouring county – tomorrow and am having to leave Grace and Jo here. However, I shall probably get home most weekends. I must close now and see to my packing but I will write again as soon as possible.

Please give our love to the children and again we thank you both for all you are doing for us.

Dinah's sixth birthday party at 54 Forest Avenue on 27 December 1940.

Janet Matthews to Grace Mathews

28 December 1940   Trelawny, Glendale, Ohio

Of course you will want to know about Clifford's Christmas. I think he had a happy day, with the high spot being the radiogram from his family.

On the Monday before Christmas, all four boys and Mr Matthews and I went to Cincinnati and the boys did their shopping for one another and their friends. We all met for luncheon at an hotel and had a hearty and hilarious meal. In the late afternoon there was a Sunday School party, with a movie and candy and fruit for refreshments.

Christmas Eve, Clifford and Mr Matthews and I went to children's Christmas service, which was very appealing with a children's choir singing the old familiar carols and dressed in red vestments, looking quite angelic (although there were plenty of spoiled brats among them).

We then went about delivering presents and came home to find the Christmas tree in place and set about decorating it. The boys did all the work and I sat back and gave unsolicited advice! The result was the prettiest tree we ever had, I think.

After dinner, we took our presents to the colored family which had been assigned to us by the community nurse. That is always fun because those poor people have no Christmas cheer, being extremely hard up and having a large family of children.

Then, all very tired, we went home and Mr Matthews read 'The Night Before Christmas', which is an old family tradition. Then everyone hung up their stockings and Clifford went to bed. The rest of us attended the midnight service, but Clifford was so sleepy after his busy day that he agreed that he had better go to bed.

Next morning we were up fairly early to examine the stockings, which were full of pencils, candy, soap, toothbrushes and little silly toys. After breakfast we marched into the living room for packages. Clifford had a nice pile as all aunts and uncles had remembered him as well as our boys. There were books, flashlights, airplanes, soldiers, neckties, handkerchiefs etc and a bicycle, which we decided he would enjoy because all the boys his age have them and he had spoken of enjoying his at home. Just as he was finishing the opening of his gifts, Sheila and Dinah came and he showed them all the things and then he went down to Wyoming to see what they had been given.

At dinner we had Mr Matthews's mother and the oldest sister and two refugee friends of theirs – we always have the same things for Christmas dinner, turkey, cranberries and plum pudding. After dinner Clifford rode his bicycle and by the end of the day he had ridden seven miles! So he was once more ready for bed.

Yesterday, as you know, was Dinah's birthday and the Strohmengers invited him to supper. He says he taught the girls to play football and then they had a party ending with ice-cream and birthday cake. In the evening Clifford was invited to a dance in Glendale. He said it was great fun but his feet hurt from dancing so much. Today he is playing quietly with some of the boys. Vacation will be over the day after New Year's and it will seem very tame with all the boys in school again.

His first school report has come home and as we expected all the grades are excellent. Our greatest problem is to keep him from getting spoiled by too much publicity and attention. A number of the English children have had their heads rather badly turned by all the fuss that has been made over them. The sad part is that it makes them unpopular with their classmates as well as with grown-ups. You have done such a splendid job with your boy's bringing up that we are anxious not to have him go home to you badly spoiled. So we have turned down all offers of newspapers, magazines and radio stations for interviews, feeling that they would not be good for him. I hope you will approve of our attitude. Americans love foreigners and always make a great fuss over them for a while and then forget all about them when someone new turns up. We are funny people with lots of faults but you could not help but like Americans if you could see the warm-hearted way they have treated the British children. I find that even the roughest boys are thoughtful and friendly to Clifford.

Winter has set in here but we hope to go to Florida for February. We have a cottage there and Don and Clifford can take their school books and be tutored. They would have lots of sun and we have found with our own children that they keep well up with their school work and avoid the coughs and colds that so often crop up at that time of year.

I think the subject of confirmation will come up in Lent. Most of Clifford's friends here will be confirmed this year. I imagine you might prefer to have him wait until he goes home, but if you wish it he could join the classes here. We want to do whatever you would like best.

Thank you for your Christmas greetings. We all fervently hope that 1941 will be a better year than 1940 – it could hardly be worse.

When I read over my letters they always sound stuffy. It is partly because I want to report seriously to you about your boy. Really, we aren't quite so dull. We have a cheerful and happy time and I hope Clifford can make it clear to you that we are not as serious as I sound.

With kindest regards to you all – especially Jo who must be a fascinating baby from all the accounts we hear.

Grace Mathews to Janet and Bill Matthews

January 1941   Runcton, Chichester, Sussex

I know that you will forgive me for delegating to my husband the answering of your letters. Although he insists that he is a very busy man, he has had much more time than I have during the last few months, or perhaps his power of concentration is greater than mine under the present circumstances.

My life in the last few months seems to have been one wild dash trying to keep house. I lost my only helper and the laundry was bombed out. We had been housing friends from the town and eventually we were squeezed out entirely from our home by the avalanche of refugees after the weekend blitz of Southampton. We were fortunate enough to get a small bungalow in the village where one of my sisters lives, some twelve miles away. Petrol is rationed but my husband is still able to run a car because of his job, so we felt that we should be the ones to make room. This has all been combined with dashes day and night to the shelter. On top of all that, my husband has now been moved permanently (as far as we know) to Chichester, a cathedral town near the South Coast. We are at present staying in a small village two miles out of the town, recuperating and getting ready to face yet another move.

Now I must try to express my thanks to you and Mr Matthews for your great kindness in sheltering Clifford – no words can ever thank you enough. It has been a most anxious and heartbreaking time for his father and I parting with our darlings, but events have proved that we were right to send them to you. Happenings here must remain forever in the minds of even the most stolid among us.

Yours and Mrs Strohmenger's letters reached us just as we were having a very trying period and I cannot tell you what happiness and strength they gave us. The courage of the people who have lost everything is amazing. They have only the clothes they stand up in, but they are only too thankful that they have come through. We have just received your letter of 4 December and it makes us very proud to know that Clifford is facing news as we would like him to. I often wondered if we could bring him up mannish enough with three sisters, but he was a good boy and so kind with his baby sister. She misses him very much and is always talking of him. I hope to be able to send some snaps along soon. I'm sure Cliff will think Jo has grown, though it has been very difficult to get the necessary diet for her. New-laid eggs have been unobtainable and milk is very scarce, but that is now better.

What a coincidence it is that your husband should play the fiddle. My husband also has one, as Cliff has no doubt told you, and he conscientiously attended lessons for seven years but he is always reluctant to play when asked. We used to take part in concerts arranged by our local tennis club and found it was at rehearsals that we had the greatest fun.

How I would have loved to have a glimpse of the boys together at

Xmas. You mentioned that you and your husband are poor sub-stitutes for Cliff's parents – our only worry is that you seem to be making such a good job of it that he may not want to come home. We are, however, more than delighted to know that he is with a family as understanding and good-hearted as yours obviously is.

The Hun planes are flying overhead, making for the north apparently, which is very distracting so I will end by wishing you all a very happy and prosperous New Year.

Clifford Mathews to his parents

27 January 1941   Trelawny, Glendale, Ohio

I am so sorry I have not written before but I have been very busy studying for the exams which start on Wednesday. I am in the 7th Grade at school and boy is the work easy. You probably will doubt it but I can do the Latin and Algebra that Don is doing in Grade 10. I got to thinking the other evening and I decided that I should have some more work to do and so I am going to take Latin. I don't think it has ever been done before in the 7th Grade.

I have been elected as secretary of the class. We have Home Room meetings every Monday and we discuss things of interest. Today for the third time a dance was discussed. Eventually it was put off until next meeting. I think that's just typical. They do a lot of talking and never get anywhere. They looked quite disgusted when I moved that a committee be appointed to fix and arrange the date for it. It's just the same in Social Science. The boys and girls have so very different ideas about things than I do. At first I tried to argue but I gave it up and have learned to shut up. But they take it in good humour and are very nice about it.

By the way, I have just been initiated as a member of the Chi-Rho Club. It was the worst time I have had for a long time. The initiation is just to see that you are a good sport – they make you bend over and get swatted a couple of hundred times and pour molasses and paste down inside your shirt and all over your face and by the time you are finished you feel pretty fed up. But I am proud of my little red pin and the meetings are loads of fun. I am feeling fine and have put on about five pounds at least. I hope you all received your presents.

John Mathews to Janet and Bill Matthews

29 January 1941

c/o The Petroleum Board, Kingsham Road,
Chichester, Sussex

We have just received Mrs Matthews's very nice letter of 28 December. I may tell you that we look forward to them very much and they act like a tonic to both Mrs Mathews and I. By the way, that 'Mrs Mathews' sounds ridiculously formal to me when writing to two people who are acting as the very gracious parents of our only son, and therefore I shall allude to my better half in future as Grace.

We were glad to hear you had a happy time at Christmas and Master Clifford seems to have done *very well indeed*. It was nice of you to suggest that the high spot for him was the receipt of our radiogram, but if I had been in Cliff's shoes I think the receipt of that bicycle would have been my high spot. What a lucky young blighter he is. He has never had so much for Christmas in his life before and he must have been excited about it all. He used to lose his appetite over here if he was over-excited – I wonder if he did at Christmas. He told us in his last letter that he had so many things to do that he could not make up his mind which to try, and that he was actually looking forward to his return to school. We were glad to hear that anyway because it shows that he is happy there.

I notice that you all had breakfast before going into the living room to the parcels. Over here, the children seem to wake at dawn, and down they rush to see what they have and after that there is no rest for anyone in the terrific din that goes on until breakfast time. Father in the meantime makes a cup of tea supposedly for mother, but actually he is dying for two or three strong cups himself, having probably drunk quite a lot of beer the previous evening. Beer by the way is a sort of national beverage over here where the menfolk are concerned; my father tells me that it is much weaker nowadays than it was in his young days. I think that must be the case because it is quite the exception to see a man, even of the labouring classes, under the influence of drink nowadays.

It was awfully kind of Mr and Mrs Strohmenger to give the girls such a good time, especially with Dinah's birthday coming so soon on top of Christmas. We have just received a photograph of the three children from Wyoming and they look splendid. Cliff's tie was immediately admired by his cousin Hugh, in fact our children are envied by all their cousins over here, and we almost hate to tell them what a wonderful time Cliff and the girls are having, but they always want to know all about them so we endeavour to tone down our recitals as much as possible. Of course, everyone tries to cheer us up by telling us, 'Oh my dears, they will never want to come home again.'

Before I continue, have you received any of our letters yet? We always write to you and the children at least once in about ten days. I know we have not received all yours or Cliff's. Of Cliff's little parcels which he apparently sent over for Christmas the stockings arrived ('corn in Egypt') but whatever else he sent is apparently missing. That is the fortune of war I suppose and that's why I told the rascal not to spend money on things for us.

Your snaps arrived with your letter and we thought them lovely. (Grace says that if she were writing the letter, she would have said that *you* looked lovely. That might be all very well as one woman to another, but personally I do not want Mr Matthews coming over with a gun again just yet. Not looking for me anyway.)

We are definitely delighted to know of your attitude regarding the attention of press reporters, broadcasting etc in connection with Cliff. We absolutely and entirely agree with you on this. Not so much because of what the children might be like when they return but because while they are in America they have a job of work to do, and when they return we want them to leave behind a host of good friends and well-wishers. Those foster parents in America who may be allowing English children to become spoilt dominating little brats are doing both the children and their country a disservice.

You make us blush with shame when you talk of the 'splendid job' we have done in bringing up that young fellow. Actually we were rather slack, I'm afraid, especially on the spiritual side, so the question of confirmation is rather difficult. I have always felt that no child should be confirmed into any faith until that child is old enough to understand exactly what the service means. On the other hand, Cliff always struck me as much older in his line of thought than his actual age, and therefore we should like you to come to a decision yourselves. There is always the possibility that if it is delayed until he comes back to this country he might be averse to the idea of going through the ceremony with strangers in a strange church. Would you please talk it over with him, and whatever you decide we shall be quite happy.

You say your letters are stuffy: the truth is they are quite the contrary I assure you, and they are actually the wine of life to us.

Of course we still like to think that we have a sense of humour, and the more fun you can squeeze into your letters the better. There is not really much to scream with laughter about over here just now.

Well, by the time this arrives I suppose you will be sunning yourselves in Florida. The experiences that boy is having should enable him to write a book about it all, which is not a bad idea by the way. Over here the weather has been very cold. I use the car quite a bit and travelling has been anything but pleasant. I think I could have enjoyed it better if I had had some of the children on a toboggan tied to the back of the car as I did last year. Another thing which makes travelling in bad weather anything but pleasant now is the absence of all signposts.[1] The other day I did half an hour's hard driving only to find myself back where I started. However spring must be on its way, and we look forward to it despite Hitler's threat of invasion with thousands of planes. One of his night bombers was brought down in the sea near us a few nights back. It was a jet black night, and a few seconds before the bomber crashed the fighter plane that brought him down passed over our house with its navigation lights showing. Those boys certainly have plenty of nerve and my gosh they need it. We haven't any air raid shelter here and sometimes when we begin to look for the safest spot in the bungalow nothing looks very safe. Grace is very good, in fact I think her nerves are better than mine. It must be rotten having a woman in the house who gets the jitters every time the siren goes, but the great majority of the weaker!! sex are wonderful.

Another royal proclamation has been announced calling up men in the eighteen to forty-two group, so I shall register shortly. I don't suppose I shall have the luck to get into anything, though, because the Petroleum Board will not release me. *Such* an important fellow y'know. The trouble is that the salaries paid are not keeping up with the terrific increase in prices. Never mind, we eat and drink so why worry.

I have just heard on the radio news that Admiral Knox,[2] giving evidence before the Senate on the Lease Lend Bill,[3] stated that the

---

[1] Street names and signposts in Britain were removed at the end of May 1940 and, in rural areas, were not restored until the middle of 1943.

[2] William Franklin Knox, 1874–1944, Secretary of the Navy. Oddly perhaps, he was a colonel rather than an admiral.

[3] This was passed by Congress on 11 March 1941. The Lend-Lease Act empowered President Roosevelt to supply warships, munitions, fuel oil and other goods to Britain without payment in cash. Churchill described lend-lease as a 'monument of generous and far-seeing statesmanship'.

Huns were preparing to launch an attack on us within sixty days and that they would use gas. I hope his information is incorrect. Personally I think it is, because obviously if the Hun started that game over here then we would reciprocate. Well, we shall see.

I think it is time I ended, so please accept our best wishes and once again our deep gratitude for your interest and care of our son and heir. Which reminds me, he does not tell us enough in his letters. Please give him a terrific thrashing from me and tell him we expect an improvement.

Janet Matthews to Grace Mathews

30 January 1941   Trelawny, Glendale, Ohio

Your letter came through in record-breaking time – three weeks and three days. We were so glad to have the pictures of you and Mr Mathews. We happened to have a gathering of a few friends here the night your letter came and we proudly showed the picture of Cliff's parents and everyone agreed that you look very attractive, just as Cliff's family should look.

As to your fears that the children might never want to go home, I think you can dismiss them – certainly as far as Cliff is concerned! We fully realise that he is just a loan. While we want his life to be full and interesting and enjoyable, we also want him to think of us as his very special friends – sort of American headquarters – but not in any way as rivals for his affection for you and his father. We talk of you every day and we try to think how you would want things done. I know how you must feel and we are trying to strike a good balance. I would cheerfully murder anyone who tried to win my own boys away from me!

I think you would be interested in the relationship that has grown up between Don and Clifford. They each have their own friends and do not actually play together very much but when they are together they are most congenial and have their little jokes. Sometimes Don gives Cliff a bit of fatherly advice about school and sometimes Cliff does little favors for Don. I have never heard them exchange a cross word! Don has the best disposition in the family, due partly to having two older brothers to put him in his place – but for some reason he seems to have no desire to take it out on younger children. He is enormously fond of Cliff and always telling me of his good work at school, his popularity with the boys etc. When Don's orchestra played before the whole school, Cliff got home first and said, 'Don was the whole show, everyone liked him best.'

Happily for us all, Clifford really is the most tactful child I have ever seen. Never once has he criticised any of us or Americans and I know we must seem strange to him. The result is that we can discuss the differences in English and American table manners, school systems, clothing etc in the friendliest way without anyone trying to prove that one system is superior to the other. Most Americans (including my ignorant self) have thought of the English as an arrogant lot who despise and look down on Americans – not a very good foundation for friendship. We also think that the British picture all Americans as noisy and ill-mannered with no fine feelings. So it is a distinct shock to us to find that there are all kinds of Englishmen just as there are all sorts of Americans – and there is a lot to be said for them both. Our children, entirely due to their admiration for Cliff, are going to avoid the mistakes of their parents and be most kindly disposed towards the British.

We send you congratulations on the marvelous spirit you all have and hope that your victory will come soon. If we could only get going on our helping campaign it would be nice, but we really don't have much control over the matter and maybe a great deal more is going on than we realise.

Clifford Mathews to his parents

2 February 1941   Trelawny, Glendale, Ohio

I received your presents last Thursday and was very pleased to get them because as Sheila had already received hers I was afraid she was going to be the only lucky one.

I rode down with two of my friends to Wyoming to see Sheila and Dinah. I am afraid you will not be able to understand Dinah when she comes home, she has an awful accent. Her pet expression is 'Oh fooey'. When I got there they were curling hair as Gloria has her piano lessons this afternoon and Sheila has her dancing lessons this evening.

The Chi-Rho Club to which I belong is giving a dance tonight. The orchestra was hired and arrangements were made but the girls were forgotten! We sent the invitations out yesterday only to find that only nine of the 24 invited can come. There'll be a rush. There are 25 boys. Incidentally the orchestra we are hiring is the one that Don plays in. He certainly is good. He played in front of the school during auditorium period the other morning and they went crazy over it.

Well, I must close now.

John Mathews to Janet and Bill Matthews

15 February 1941   Chichester, Sussex

We received your letter dated 30 January yesterday, so although my letter to you took only a little over three weeks your reply beats all records to date. I wonder if you realise just how much your letters mean to us. When I get to the office in the morning, my chief storekeeper grins and says, 'An American letter on your desk, sir.' That starts the morning very well indeed, and I regret to say that business is at a complete standstill until I have thoroughly scanned the contents. When I arrive home I say to Grace, 'Guess what I have,' but it's no good, she knows immediately. Believe me, they are a ray of sunshine in our lives.

We received the photograph of the children. It was very good of you to cooperate with Mrs Strohmenger in this and we could not have wished for a nicer Xmas present. The three musketeers look so happy and healthy. I have purchased an album specially to keep all the photographs and snaps from America, and have started it with this one. Grace and Jo are going to have their photograph taken next week, if I can persuade Grace to sit. She is as shy of having her photograph taken as she is of writing letters. But whereas I have every excuse for not having mine taken, she on the contrary takes a very good picture, at least I think so.

We are very pleased that Don and Cliff get along well. Obviously you have a gift for mothering boys and managing them. So many mothers would have made every effort to see that their boy spent all his spare time with the evacuee, with disastrous results. I imagine you have allowed them to make their own friendships so that when they do come together they can have fun and a friendly chat without getting on each other's nerves. I remember when I was fifteen I thought of boys of twelve as mere babies, and as for spending time with them, not on your life.

I would love to hear Cliff in a discussion with you all about the various differences between the two nationalities. I expect he often shrugs his shoulders and my recollection is that usually meant that his reply, if given, would be embarrassing to himself or to the listener. When I first wrote to you I mentioned that I hoped he would be a good ambassador and he seems to have made a job of it if it is he who has persuaded you that we are not 'an arrogant lot who despise and look down on Americans'. I assure you that of the great many people of my acquaintance, the majority, on reading your remark, would say, 'How extraordinary'. They simply wouldn't understand why you might think us arrogant. Mind you, in the old days the Englishman was taught as a boy at school that one Englishman was as good as four foreigners, whereas in these enlightened days we only think one Englishman as good as three Italians or two Germans. You see what I mean, we are improving all the time. Of course, in the old days, we won more battles than we do just now.

Seriously though, I think that better education for the masses and improved facilities for travelling abroad will, as time goes on, remove most of these fallacious ideas which one nation now has about another. I will say that as far as America is concerned, you have probably gained financial returns from your film industry, but that same industry has given the rest of the world such a complex confusion of ideas of what the ordinary American man in the street is like that the average foreigner has a picture of Americans which is just a darn shame and grossly unfair to you people. Again, the visitors who go from this country to yours, and vice versa, are often quite erroneously taken to be a fair criterion on which to base the standard of a whole nation.

We are going all American in this household. We have been listening to an anthology of American poems and songs on the wireless this evening – I listen to WRUL Boston, the only American station I can get really well nowadays – and I read American books. But to go from the sublime to the ridiculous, can you tell me why Americans, sorry *some* Americans, call us 'Limeys'?

Well, I must close. I have to be on duty all night tomorrow fire-bomb watching. We all take our turn on that job. I shall sit in my office playing chess with my chief storekeeper unless an Alert sounds. I'm all right, but it is a beastly nuisance for Grace because she knows nobody here and spends the night alone with Jo. Another grudge I shall have against Hitler.

Grace Mathews to Jean and Warren Strohmenger

18 February 1941   'Cassio', South Avenue, Bognor Regis, Sussex

 We have just received your letters dated 10 December and 4 January, and believe me your letters are a great source of pleasure to my husband and to me. You gave the children a great time at Christmas and we thought it more than kind of everyone to treat them as though they were your own. We can just imagine them with their presents. Dinah especially, I expect, was tremendously thrilled. Then there was her birthday. You certainly have been busy, and as I have had the four of them I can appreciate better than most perhaps just how much extra work it has meant for you.

Mrs Matthews told us in a recent letter that Sheila could not go with them to a museum because she was studying hard for exams, so I see you have carried out your threat to make her do her homework. I'm glad to know that you are, because she had a good deal of leeway to make up from not being able to get to school very often over here after the war started. Even when they did get to school the children were more often than not too tired from a sleepless night in the air raid shelter to give proper attention to their lessons. As time goes on and rumours of invasion here become more prevalent, whether there is anything in them or not, we are more and more thankful that we sent the children to you.

I have just read through your December letter again, and the bit about the children racing around upstairs reminds me of old times. I used to send them off to bath before going to bed and very shortly after I used to hear a terrific noise emanating from the bathroom, from which I knew they were up to their old games. They used to sit on the edge of the bath and slide down into the water with a tremendous splash. Half the bathwater used to go on the floor so I hope they have not initiated Gloria into the game for your sake.

We are very near several aerodromes here and perhaps that is why we are quieter, by which I mean fewer actual bombs dropping. We get as many as six air raid warnings during a day and night, and enemy planes over by the dozen at night. Very few come over in daylight. I imagine that is because of their experiences last year when our boys brought down as many as 185[1] in twenty-four hours.

---

[1] A figure claimed by the RAF on 15 September 1940, now celebrated as Battle of Britain Day. The actual German losses were subsequently discovered to have been no more than sixty aircraft.

We were glad the children were able to do something for 'Bundles for Britain' and, from what we have seen, anything that they sent will be welcomed over here. Certainly if anyone over here prior to the war ever felt that your feelings in America were far from friendly towards us, they must have revised their ideas in the last year. You people couldn't have done much more for us if we had been fellow Americans. Of course we like to look upon you as cousins anyway. I wonder if we ever shall actually meet after this business is over. I sincerely hope so, even if it is only long enough for me to thank you personally for all you are doing.

Clifford Mathews to his parents

February 1941   766 Bay Esplanade, Clearwater, Florida

I am writing to you for the first time from Florida. We are on the side of the state facing the Gulf of Mexico. It is extremely hot here and the grass and the flowers will not grow unless they are watered thoroughly once a day. The trees are mostly palms.

I have a little dinghy and a tiny little half-horse power motor which I run most of the time. It is a wonderful little motor and it gets me around quite fast. I have named it HMS *Totton* and the words are painted in bold red letters on the back of the boat. Yesterday Mr Matthews bought me a fishing rod and I have been fishing all day long. I was very lucky this morning and caught five beautiful spotted trout. However this afternoon has not been so good. I have just finished cleaning them, so if this letter smells fishy blame the trout.

Last Sunday afternoon we went by boat to Tarpon Springs, a Greek colony which has the largest sponge fishing fleet in the world. They fish for the sponges in the Gulf of Mexico. I saw one of the divers in his diving suit.

Don could not come down with us because he had a lot of school work to do but he will be here two weeks from today. We were on the train for 24 hours coming from Cincinnati, my longest trip on a train, 1,000 miles.

I am getting very sunburned but it is not quite warm enough to swim yet.

Well, must end now and just say that Sheila and Dinah are fine.

Jean Strohmenger to Grace and John Mathews

11 March 1941   54 Forest Avenue, Wyoming, Ohio

We received your letters dated 18 February today and were all so glad to hear from you. Dinah was complaining because hers wasn't as long as the rest of ours and because Gloria didn't get one, but I told her that the letters were for all of us and that we got longer ones because we wrote longer letters to you, so that seemed to take care of the subject. This letter was the first one that the censors had touched. They cut out a paragraph in which you apparently told about an air battle.

You were saying in your letter that you wondered if we would ever meet. I'm quite sure we shall. We were planning on taking a trip but the war changed our plans. Warren says that he would like to see things right after the war, and then see how it will be built up later on. I think the children will keep after you until you have a trip over here. I don't intend to be bragging but I think the girls have learned to like America a lot. I wonder if you realise how much more they have been Americanised than they would have been had they come over with you, for instance. They have learned to accept things in a hurry, whereas if you were with them so many of the habits of England would still be carried on. And, too, they have been invited into the homes of all the folks around, to parties and such, where people coming in as strangers wouldn't have been accepted as quickly. It was quite a strain on them at first, but being young they soon got into the swing of things. Just this evening, a boy in Sheila's class (Judge Gorman's son) called and invited Sheila to a dance he is having at his home this coming Friday evening. Sheila was quite pleased as it is the first boy's party to which she has been invited. Gloria is invited to a birthday luncheon on Saturday. Last weekend it was Dinah and Gloria going to a movie and dessert party. I keep quite busy getting in birthday presents and getting to all the parties to deliver and call for, never to mention getting hair washed and bodies bathed.

The girls had a big laugh about your memories of sliding down the bathtub. As soon as I read the paragraph I inserted a warning that I didn't want anything like that happening upstairs here, so they said that they couldn't do it in our tub because it is small and is surrounded by wall on three sides. So, you see, they had had the idea.

Clifford Mathews on holiday, 1941.

Janet Matthews to Grace and John Mathews

18 March 1941   766 Bay Esplanade, Clearwater, Florida

When your 15 February letter arrived yesterday I felt very ashamed that I had not answered your last one yet. I really enjoy writing to you and my excuse for being so remiss is the usual one – pretty busy.

Now to answer some of your questions. First, British–American relations. I think we are like relations, who quarrel among themselves and find many things to criticise, but let a common enemy appear and we find that we are both pretty good fellows after all and like one another more than we realised. At present in the United States to say that a man is anti-British is only one small step lower than to accuse him of being pro-Nazi. The admiration for the English is universal.

For some reason I had never heard the expression 'Limey' – but I find that everyone else has and the explanation given to me is as follows. The men in the merchant marine of your country were given lime juice to supplement a rather restricted diet. I suppose it supplied those now-famous little fellows called vitamins although they were probably not known as such at the time.

Janet Matthews in Florida.

The film industry, I fear, has thought more of making money than of painting us in a sympathetic light. At the moment they are putting out a wave of historical pictures, which are an improvement over the modern themes. We recently saw a film called *So Ends Our Night* dealing with the problems of Jewish refugees without passports, which we were all very enthusiastic about. There wasn't a glamour girl anywhere in sight. I can hardly take another exotic heroine – probably because no sturdy, slightly athletic creature like myself could ever be glamorous or exotic – the old green-eyed monster will rear its ugly head.

Explaining our school system to you will require a more enlightened person than I. When we get home I will ask Mr Slade our school superintendent to write and give you more information than I can. I think our American schools are less formal than English ones, and discipline, I fear, is not as good. Supposedly we strive to make the child self-reliant, to make him think, to help him to have an inquiring mind by stimulating his interest in worthwhile things. I have heard it said that a young Englishman is far better educated than the average American youth. I have no way of checking this and I merely put it in as a graceful bouquet!

We go back to Glendale tomorrow and a pretty reluctant group we are for a blizzard is raging in the west and no doubt Cincinnati will be cold and snowy. It has never warmed up here properly this year but we have had lots of sun. Cliff is beautifully brown even after he washes. We have had very few swims, but Cliff and I are real enthusiasts and go in when the rest of them think it too cool.

Don and Cliff do not seem to care about spending much time with the other children available, so I assume that they find each other amusing. They know a small boy who owns a sailboat, which is perfect for the bay in front of our house. They have been cultivating him of late to use his boat. Yesterday I noticed that Edward was perched on the bow deck in lonely splendor and Cliff and Don were having a wonderful time with the tiller and ropes. When they came in I asked them if they shouldn't sometimes let Edward take over. 'Oh, gosh no,' they said, 'he doesn't know anything about sailing.' I don't know where the home team got this profound knowledge of sailing, but if Edward is satisfied why should I complain?

We have had some lively competition in shuffle board and a game called croquet, which they pronounce 'crokee' and tell us, by the way, is an English game. It seems to be a cross between golf and croquet à la Américain. The boys are one team called the Minnows, the men are the Marlins, the women being called the Willets. (Do you know willets? – they are a singularly large and ungraceful beach bird.) We keep a daily record and it changes rapidly as one game changes your standing. The day the Minnows dropped into last place was a serious disaster for the boys. They practised like mad and are now on top of the heap. Cliff is also catching on quickly to baseball and seems to like it, which is fortunate as every small boy will be playing when we get home. Maybe you've noticed that he is a natural athlete. We certainly have.

We look forward to a picture of Mrs Mathews and Jo. It *is* a frightful ordeal to 'sit' for a picture, but Cliff would love it!

Thank you for your 'swell' letters. Best wishes from us all.

John Mathews to Janet and Bill Matthews

4 April 1941   Hamilton, Hewarts Lane, Bognor Regis, Sussex

We have just received your nice long letter and the snaps. You all look very fit and brown. We cannot imagine Florida being cool, especially too cool to bathe. I expect Cliff found the water about the same as it would be here in mid-summer. We think we are lucky if the sea water becomes warm enough not to make us gasp when we plunge in. We try to teach the youngsters to take a header straight in when they first enter the water, otherwise they are inclined to do a very slow march up to the knees and then stand and shiver. I expect Cliff has told you all about our Sunday trips to the sea. Cliff and I used to have a swimming race and I often had Sheila and Dinah on my back. With the run of fourteen miles through the New Forest, the bathing and games, and then the run back in the evening, we had happy times in those days. The very last day we had there together, a mine or large unexploded bomb blew up right opposite where we were on the beach. There is a perfect bathing beach at Felpham near where we are now staying and where we used to go to spend some of our holidays. We shall not be able to do any swimming there this year, worse luck, because we are not allowed on the beach. Can you imagine how annoying that is going to be on a blazing hot day? Never mind, maybe we shall all bathe there together one day in happier times. Which reminds me, if they don't ease up on this taxation business we shall not be able to afford any holidays.

Grace, Jo and I went for a walk around the lanes this evening and picked up some primroses and violets. The wild flowers are just blooming. I have put two or three primroses and violets in the envelope so that you may have a sniff of old England.

Well, here we are still alive and kicking. As usual there is an air raid warning on while I write this letter, but despite Hitler and his satellites my better half is in bed and sound asleep, trying to retain some of the beauty which the ravages of war strain are endeavouring to mar. This war is going to have its advantages because, when it is over, any of us who look about fifty years older than we should will be able to say, 'Yes, but look at the terrific strain we've been through.' I'm one of them, my hirsute adornment has heard the story about the rats leaving the sinking ship, I think; it is coming out so fast that it nearly stops the water from draining from the bathtub.

I was at a sea coast town some miles east of here the other day and just after I arrived at our depot a Hun dived through the low cloud and dropped a stick of HEs and then turned and did a spot of machine gunning. It's quite a thrill while it lasts. Tell Cliff that SWT[1] took a hit the other day and some employees were killed and injured. The point in question is not far from where his Grandma and Grandpa live so he will know where I mean. The old people are all right though a bit shaken.

Last month we posted you a special sort of greeting card. An association of parents has been formed in this country among those people who have sent their children to the USA. The association is called 'The Kinsmen' and it has been formed with the idea of sending through *The Seagull Post* a general greeting from parents over here to foster parents in the USA, phrased in a manner which will convey just how we feel about what you are doing for us. I believe a copy of the original 'Greeting' is to be sent to Mrs Roosevelt and to other famous Americans who have done a great deal for the children.

The idea of the association came from a Mrs Bemrose of Derby. She is an old friend of an American, Mrs Beatrice Warde, of the American Outpost in Britain. They, with the assistance of members of the American Committee for the Evacuation of Children, got out a scheme. The association will endeavour to smooth over difficulties experienced by parents, such as the question of the import duty on anything sent by parents to their children in the States. I feel tremendously honoured because at the initial meeting held in London, which I was unable to attend, a letter which I had sent to Mrs Bemrose was read to the gathering, and in the minutes of the meeting which I have just received was said to express the feelings of the whole group towards the American Committee. I could hardly get my hat on this morning.

Well, I have some more letters to write tonight so I must end. Should I fail to thank you for what you are doing for us each time I write it is simply that I don't want to bore you with repetition, and not that we are taking things for granted.

[1] South Western Tar.

Jocelyn ('Jo') and Grace Mathews in Bognor Regis.

John Mathews to Clifford Mathews

9 May 1941   Hamilton, Hewarts Lane, Bognor Regis, Sussex

Hallo you old rascal, how are you? You must be looking like the fat boy of Peckham if all I hear about your putting on weight is true. Can you still run, or do you puff along under the terrific load?

Talking of running, what did you do about the Hamilton Track Meet? I hope you had a crack at one or two events. It would be a great experience for you, and although you might be up against some stiff opposition, as I have always told you it matters *nothing* whether you win or lose as long as you do your best, and having done that you have a good race.

Sheila is getting to be quite a baseball player apparently and I hear she is practising tennis pretty assiduously. Do you play tennis? By the way, does it strike you that the fact that I have to ask these questions just shows what a lot you *don't* tell us in your letters, and if you send me another letter like the one I am now looking at I will catch the next clipper over and completely spiflicate you. This is the sort of thing you have written, 'We have dark room in the cellar, and Mr Matthews is going to equip it for me for developing and printing of my pictures. Well I'll soon but for the present I am paying all my attention to Charlie McCarthy who has just come on the air.'[1] Charlie McCarthy my foot. You will please to write me a long letter next time telling me all about everything ... or else.

Well, what do you think about the night fighters over here? 120 down this month in eight days and nights. Nice work, eh?

My own letter writing has gone to seed today and I don't seem to be able to concentrate, so I will make this a short letter and end by saying Charlie McCarthy is just coming on the air ...

So long, old fellow. Don't worry about us over here, everything is just fine.

Janet Matthews to Grace and John Mathews

May 1941   Trelawny, Glendale, Ohio

Last weekend Bill and I went to Iowa to see our big boys. They were fine and we had a chance to look over the girl who has so completely bewitched our Billy. She was so attractive and well-mannered that we came home feeling that we were very lucky parents. She not only is an honor grade student but helps with the housework at home, where there are two boarders to be fed, and seems to find time to have some fun on the side. We wonder how 'B' was smart enough to select such a model girl.

In our absence, Cliff went to visit David Peck and Don stayed with one of his friends. They tell me that Don was constantly going to the Pecks to see how Cliff was getting along. I mention this not to show you that Don is a nice boy, but because it shows how fond he is of your boy. Don is at a selfish age and would not have given Cliff a thought if he hadn't wanted to. The only sad part of the story is that the weather was cold and Cliff did not have enough blankets and caught cold – his first since coming here. As he had a little fever, I put him to bed for a few days and he recovered in time to enjoy the weekend. He was very good and amused himself with the radio and books most of the time. One day I put a thermometer in his mouth and then had to answer the telephone. Of course I forgot about my patient and when I went back twelve minutes later he was reading a newspaper with the thermometer still in his mouth. He and Don thought this was a huge joke on an absent-minded old lady.

[1] The dummy used by the popular American ventriloquist Edgar Bergen, father of the actress Candice Bergen.

One day while Cliff was taking a rest I played some tennis. I like to dress comfortably for the game so I had on shorts, woolen socks, dirty Keds and hair blowing. Right in the midst of the game in walked the case worker looking like a spring flower, pale blue silk dress and a cute little hat with pink flowers poised over one eye. It was annoying to have her find Cliff sick for the very first time and his guardian in a wringing perspiration. However, she was so nice and looked so dainty and attractive that I softened toward her. She really isn't such a bad egg. It must be a rather thankless job going into strange homes and tactfully finding out how people are treating their charges. She left me with the feeling that she was satisfied that all was well here. You see how it is, a little flattery and I fall.

You will be amused to hear that Cliff has taken a fancy to a girl. She is a nice little girl too, apparently well thought of by both boys and girls. He took her to a movie with David Peck and another little girl. They play baseball in the evening sometimes. Of course, even this slight show of interest in a girl has caused a bit of teasing from Don's group and I really think Cliff rather enjoys it. It makes him feel so grown up. Why on earth do young things want to be old? They don't know when they're well off, do they?

You ask why our friend's family objected to his marriage in 'democratic' America. It is pretty hard to generalise in a country as large as this, but there is snobbishness of a sort everywhere. In the east, Americans are not apt to speak to strangers without a formal introduction. My brother lived in a New York apartment for two years and never spoke to any of the other tenants except perhaps to nod in the elevator. As you go further west people are more friendly. They speak to strangers, they call you by your first name at once. They don't dress as well and they don't care how you look, they are more interested in what you are like. But everywhere money talks. Americans love prosperity. However, almost everywhere people from different walks of life inter-marry and if they don't quite make the grade the chances are that their children will. Many of our millionaires were newsboys in their youth.

Glendale, I think, is rather unique. There are a number of very rich families and lots of people who just get along and nobody seems to be conscious of which is which. Everyone is exceedingly generous with what they have. There isn't a hospital or worthy charity in the city of Cincinnati that could get along without the aid of Glendale, be it financial or in the capacity of useful board member or worker. Yet Glendale people do not mingle to any great extent with city people for purely social purposes. They are happy among themselves. It sounds rather narrow but like all Americans they travel a great deal and so do not live entirely to themselves. I can be enthusiastic about Glendale because I am an outsider, having gotten into their midst by marriage.

We do not play very much bridge. Bill does not care for cards and I do not play enough to keep my hand in. Most of our friends play and enjoy as you do a small stake. However, we do play table tennis. We have a table at our summer camp. The boys play such a slashing game and like to stand so far back from the table that we removed a wall partition in the cottage to make room. Now if you are attempting to read in the cottage you are in constant danger of having balls hit you in the face. Bill and I are both enthusiasts, but we cannot beat our children any more except by playing doubles and they consider that a very inferior game.

We have had our first war casualty in the village. The son of a cousin of Bill's volunteered to drive an ambulance in Africa. Word came today that the ship on which he was a passenger had been sunk with all hands lost. The boy was only a few weeks older than our oldest and they were classmates at college last year.

School will be out for summer in about a month. It gets pretty hot here by June. There is going to be a music festival to end the year and both boys will sing. Our children's chorus is beautifully trained and I wish you could hear them. Our music teacher is a little man no bigger than a minute and full of energy. He is considered one of the best in the business and we are always afraid that some other school will lure him away with more gold. Our only hope is that he will think this is a nice place to bring up a family.

I will now tell you a secret. Bill is writing you a letter. I have tried to get him started for months. I said you would suspect that Cliff was visiting an illiterate and he said, 'Well, he is, isn't he?' But quite suddenly yesterday he started to concoct a letter. Instead of dashing it off and expecting you to forgive mistakes, he is going to do the thing right and it should go off some time before the end of summer. That makes him sound stodgy and he isn't at all, just shy and quiet and really a darling.

It was great that you had a short Easter holiday and I hope you had a rest from bombs. I wish we could take a turn at night watch and let our Mathews cousins sleep. But the best we can do is give your boy our affection and attention. That is such an easy job it is as nothing.

Bill Matthews to Grace and John Mathews

30 May 1941   Trelawny, Glendale, Ohio

I am afraid that I allow myself to be influenced by a theory of my own that an inarticulate person should accept that fact and give way to those who express themselves fluently. This letter is forcing an unnatural situation and is contrary to my theory and I hope the result will not be too awful. I am also afraid that when one has to begin a letter with such an excuse that it serves no purpose and merely marks the writer as a person inclined to procrastinate. Frankly, both my theory and what you will suspect are true.

My conscience has finally convinced me, however, that I cannot continue any longer enjoying the visit of your son, Cliff, and the delightful correspondence in progress between our families without participating in said correspondence to the extent of one letter at least.

Needless to say, although I have been a very silent partner, nevertheless I have been a real partner in all the thoughts and sentiments expressed in Janet's letters which, like yours to us, are in my opinion masterpieces in the art of letter-writing, namely talking on paper.

Cliff is a perfect guest and I would say the splendid ambassador that you would have him be. He has, in the comparatively short time that he has been here, made a real contribution to the life of this small village through his contemporaries who know him as a manly all-round boy ready for any situation that may arise. I am sure that you know by this time that as long as the world apparently had to get into this rotten mess, making it necessary for you to lend Cliff to someone, how happy we are to be 'that someone'.

The war situation in this country has been rather confused: 'All aid to Britain but no American convoys.' The President's address this week, which probably you heard over short wave, will do much to clarify the situation in his declaring an 'unlimited emergency'. We hope this will help the strike situation. In spite of our strikes, which have not been as serious as their publicity indicates, we are doing a good job of war material production and we will do a better one from now on. American industry is at its best when under great pressure for record production. I can say that as an outsider looking in because I have been in agriculture and out of industry for the past ten years. Management has never been very smart in the all-important matter of labor relations but I believe from now on that will be better, under the emergency.

Our government is a strong one with the best possible man at the head of it. War taxes and a controlled war economy have met with virtually no opposition. The President is very clever in the manner in which he wins public opinion through his 'fireside chats' over the radio (wireless à la Cliff) and there is little doubt that he will win his battle with the small but vocal isolationist group which calls itself 'America First'. We are a strange heterogeneous people and you must find us very hard to understand. I'm sure this war will do much to create a better understanding between Englishmen and Americans and that should strengthen us both.

We all enjoyed hearing your voices over the short wave radio this afternoon. Janet can best describe the excitement among the children, the elaborate arrangements so that we would surely hear you, and finally the narrow escape we had when we thought we were going to miss the broadcast entirely, so I will leave that for her next letter.

We are having unusually hot weather here for May. It is also extremely dry weather which borders on the serious side in our farming operations. We have been quite deficient in rainfall since last September. Cliff must think it never rains hard in the USA. He seems to be enjoying swimming this hot weather after school and on holidays between baseball games.

Since this is probably as long a letter as I have written in my entire life, I think I should stop and not waste your time reading any more. Assuring you of our great admiration of the way you are carrying on and wishing you the best of luck.

Janet Matthews to Grace and John Mathews

10 June 1941   Trelawny, Glendale, Ohio

Last Friday we had a great thrill. We listened to your voice over the radio in company with your children. But what a hair-raising time we had trying to do just that. Because we do not own a radio that will pick up short wave, Bill telephoned a local radio station and asked if they would permit us to listen on their set. They assured us that they had a very delicate instrument for picking up short wave and would like nothing better than to do something for the English children in this country. We persuaded the Strohmengers to come

63

with us so the children could be together. When we arrived at the station we found a high fence and a guard at the gate. We were very polite at first and assured the guard that we were guests and expected. But as the time for the broadcast grew closer I got really mad as I visualised us all missing you.

Finally, we were let in and heard over the air a distinctly Spanish chatter. It was then almost time for the English program to be over and we were wild. But suddenly they picked up an unmistakably British voice and almost at once we heard our British cousins being introduced. I was so excited I felt chills running up my back. We could hear pretty well although I'm afraid we missed a little, not being familiar with English as she is 'spoke' by the English. Because I always read your letters in American, as it were, I had completely forgotten that you would not slur your syllables as we do. If you have any fears that your children have forgotten you I wish you could have seen their eager little faces straining to catch every word. Afterwards they assured us that the radio did not do justice to your voices.

Our big boys come home from college in three days. 'B' will have to register for military service in July and I do not think that he will have a chance to go back to college. However, we are not thinking about that just now, it will be so good to see him. I can hardly bear to have the long arm of war reach out for our boys, but must get it into my head that they are no dearer to us than other sons are to their parents.

We expect to go to our Canadian cabin about 5 July. Our address there is Ojibway Island Post Office, Pointe-au-Baril, Ontario, Canada. Cliff is very anxious to see the Indians there. He has become very interested in Indian lore. I'm afraid that he is in for some disillusionment as the Ojibway Indians have not profited by their contact with the white man. They are dirty and shiftless, with a taste for alcohol. Gone are the feathered head-dresses and bows and arrows. However, there are some fine ones and our boys have always been interested in them and the Indians seem fond of the boys. There are some fascinating family names such as Pomajuwant and Pabuwash. I'm sure Cliff will enjoy sitting on the hotel dock and listening to their tales of adventure in the woods. They are not very talkative with grown-ups but love to spin yarns for the boys. There is a baseball team made up entirely of Indians and they are wonderfully swift and skillful at the game. The boys find them the most sports-manlike team they have ever played against. I think it is because

An envelope opened by the censor – Clifford Mathews to John Mathews, June 1941.

they play for the love of the game and the boys find it hard not to put winning above everything.

Cliff has not received any letters from his cousin Hugh,[1] but in spite of this he is going to be big-hearted and write. Don't be so polite to us, just tell us to have a letter written or anything else you would like done. We were amused when listening to the English children over the air to hear many of the parents saying, 'Darling, you must write more often.' Cliff has now set aside a definite time to write to his family and is sticking to his schedule pretty well. We told him that if he did not make his letters more informative than you describe them as being, we would have to inspect them instead of assuming that he was old enough to write without supervision. So now he comes down and tells us what he has written and we make suggestions for additions, but he still has the privacy of his own wording. I hope you will notice the improvement.

[1] Hugh Mathews, born 14 July 1924. During the war he served with 827 Squadron, Fleet Air Arm. At the end of October 1943, when he was in Canada under the Empire Air Training Scheme, he travelled to Glendale to visit the Two Ts.

Clifford by the swimming pool at Trelawny in 1941.

John Mathews to Janet and Bill Matthews

20 June 1941   Hamilton, Hewarts Lane, Bognor Regis, Sussex

Three thousand cheers and many hurrahs! (Grace looks over my shoulder and says something to the effect of, 'Don't be a blithering idiot, you can't start a letter like that.') But I do, and why? Because have we not today received a letter from the guv'nor? Yes sir, we have.

Seriously, although I don't think I have mentioned it, we have been looking forward to this letter for quite a time. Not that the letters from Mrs Matthews have lacked anything that we might want to know. Quite the contrary, we always look forward to them with great anticipation but, to be quite frank, and with the experience of a few years of married life behind us, we know that now and again what may appear to be a very nice arrangement from the viewpoint of the 'missus' may not prove to be exactly a bed of roses for the man about the house. However, Mr Matthews has very effectively dispelled any doubts we may have had on that point in his most charming letter. That 'charming' sounds awfully English. Perhaps I should have said 'swell'. Anyway, you know what I mean.

We were very bucked to know that you had received our radio message to the children and we are looking forward to Mrs Matthews's description of their excitement. You will know by this time from my last letter that we had the mortification of missing the broadcast here by a few seconds. Our main idea was to get the feeling that the children were listening at the same time, a sort of communion of the ether as it were. However, the message got across and that was the main thing.

I think I mentioned.that recently when a Heinkel was brought down near us I managed to snaffle a piece of the broken windscreen, made of something very like glass, which can, however, be shaped. I have had a ring made for Mrs Matthews and have at last sent it off, after a delay when the jeweller inscribed the wrong initials on it. Let me know if it does not fit as I have enough of the material left to make another – or a bracelet if you would prefer.

I, or rather we, can imagine (too much of the 'I' in my letters) your pleasure in discovering what a model of a perfect mate Bill Junior has chosen for himself. We have not yet experienced those pangs of doubt, but can understand the anxiety parents must feel in such matters. Perhaps we should be getting anxious, though, because we learn from Cliff that *he* has a girlfriend now. What a surprise. Old Cliff would run a mile from a girl over here, unless that is she happened to come in useful as a wicket-keeper.

My correspondence with the USA is increasing all the time. We have just had a letter from a farmer friend of the Strohmengers. Apparently Sheila has stayed with them on occasional visits and he thought we would like to know how our daughter was getting on out there. We thought it was very nice of him and his attitude was typical of the kindness which has been shown to the youngsters since they left this country.

Well, I will end by thanking you for two very interesting letters and a hope that it will not be too long before we hear from Mr Matthews again. Not that we have anything to shout about. Grace hates writing because she insists that her spelling is remarkable for its inaccuracies.

Jean Strohmenger to Grace and John Mathews

5 July 1941   54 Forest Avenue, Wyoming, Ohio

Many thanks for your Fourth of July greetings yesterday. Western Union called with the message before 8 am and started our day off with a bang. Dinah said last night that she wished she could be here for all the Fourth of Julys. At 10 am we rushed down to the corner to see the parade. The American Legion led, with the children's band which they sponsor following, all in satin costumes and with two little drum majorettes who fascinated your girls. Then the village fire department and garbage trucks and police cars and grocery trucks and autos followed, all decorated in red, white and blue and flags. There was the bicycle brigade and a prize for the best decorated bicycle. The parade ended at the Athletic Field where the contests then began. When Warren got home from his calls about 2 pm we walked down to get the girls and see if they weren't about ready for some lunch.

We did not go to the baseball game in the afternoon, but at 8 pm we went back for the evening entertainment and fireworks. First we sang to the band music. You should have seen Sheila and Dinah standing up singing 'God Bless America' and 'The Star-Spangled Banner' at the top of their lungs. (But don't worry, they still sing their English songs.) The mayor of the village of Wyoming spoke and Rev Dodson, a chaplain at one of the army camps. Last but not least were the fireworks. There were sky-rockets and pinwheels as well as the picture fireworks: a big battleship (in outline) firing blue and red cannon balls at tanks and cannons which were firing back. Then there was Niagara Falls, Two Roses, the American Flag and the like. After that we drove to the 'White Castle' and got hamburgers and hot chocolate and then home to bed.

The girls have witnessed just about all of our holidays now. They have had an American Thanksgiving, Christmas, birthdays and last, Fourth of July.

The girls will go in to the hospital to get their tonsils and adenoids out sometime this week, I think. They are looking forward to it with much enthusiasm, but I am not. Methinks Dinah will go in to one of her weeping acts, which are a little unnerving. However, we think they will be much better off after they have gotten over it all.

Jean and Warren Strohmenger with Dinah, Gloria and Sheila, 20 July 1941.

Janet Matthews to Grace and John Mathews

July 1941   Pointe-au-Baril, Ontario, Canada

The nicest thing happened! As we stepped off the train at Pointe-au-Baril they handed us the cable from you people. It was a perfect send-off for what I hope will be a 'swell' vacation.

Bill was tremendously pleased that you liked his letter. He is now saying he must think of a suitable topic and write again. I made various helpful suggestions like the 'Love Life of the House Fly', but he just withers me with a look. And by the way, why all this excitement over one letter from the old man? There is more rejoicing in heaven over one sinner ... and more praise in Bognor Regis for a single literary effort from the man of the house than for all the

Bill Matthews on the way home after a picnic, Canada 1941.

tedious epistles from the madam. I hasten to say I'm joking lest I sound really miffed. I am always trying to be funny and being taken seriously.

By the way, you say there is too much 'I' in your letters. There is certainly much too much of that same word in mine, but if we begin to worry about being properly self-effacing our letters will never get written.

All our boys are going to be with us for at least part of the time we are here and, as we have been unable to hire a man to do any of the chores which camping requires, we have persuaded Harry to stay on and work for us, taking charge of the boats, firewood, ice etc and keeping an eye on the younger boys. Cliff has Dave Peck visiting him for this month and Tom Jacobs is here while his parents are in Glendale with their oldest son, who is on furlough. Harry has assigned jobs to the boys and every morning after breakfast they put up the flags and carry in the wood. We are supervising their activities in as unobtrusive a way as possible. They have played a lot of tennis and Cliff is showing great improvement. He goes at it with terrific determination, shirt tails flying and those unruly curls on end.

Cliff is furious that word has gotten to you about his girlfriend. As a matter of fact, I think that Lonsdale has been the aggressor. She took him to the movies just a few nights before we left home. She is extremely popular with the boys and does not have to go

Glendale boys on holiday at Pointe au Baril, Ontario, Canada in 1941.
Dave Peck (left), Tom Jacobs and Clifford Mathews.

about asking for attention, so the only explanation I can think of for this unusual show of interest on her part is that she cannot resist his charm. I am afraid that quite a few of the girls think he is attractive – and there is nothing shy about the young American girl. However, he will never be allowed to get a swelled head with all the kidding from the older boys.

This is a beautiful spot and when you come to America you must see this part of the world. Our cottage stands high above the water and as you look out over the blue bay, dotted with pine-covered islands, it seems very remote from war. But only seventeen miles away is a huge munitions plant and all the Indians who looked so picturesque are actually making shells for the war.

I wish I could give you a word picture of Pointe-au-Baril so that you could visualise Cliff in his surroundings. There are some forty thousand islands in Georgian Bay, all rocky, mostly granite. Some people find them bleak but we love the rocks. They seem to change color with the rising and setting of the sun. An amazing amount of pine, scrub oak and maple and birch exists on the protected islands. Blueberries abound and they tell us that in spring there are lots of wild flowers. By the time we get here the wild iris is the only bloom left.

We live on an eleven acre island by ourselves. There is one fairly large building containing a living room, dining room, games room

71

and kitchen, and the only bathroom on the island. Bill and I sleep in a tiny sleeping bungalow.

Close by is the boy's sleeping dormitory with room for seven. There are two small bungalows for guests. Everything is very simple. We have a Delco plant and consequently electricity. This is frowned on by our friends who all use coal-oil lamps. Our reason for being so fancy is that we always have lots of boys here and several times lamps have been knocked over in the general rough housing. We became so nervous about the fire hazard that we were afraid to leave the island after dark. We do not often go out to dinner here but when we do we like to enjoy ourselves. Cooking is done with wood. Ice is cut right off the island in the winter and stored in an ice house. Once a day a boat delivers milk and another brings groceries.

If you are fond of the water, this place is the old 'veritable paradise'. You may swim, sail, canoe, row, fish, loll in the sun on the hot rocks after your swim. Well, you can see that we love it here. Then we are so fond of the Canadians. Here no one is stiff. When the local carpenter passed through Glendale, he and his wife had dinner with us and we had a lovely visit. There is a natural dignity and poise about these people that is exceedingly attractive.

How I do run on.

John Mathews to Janet and Bill Matthews

3 August 1941   Hamilton, Hewarts Lane, Bognor Regis, Sussex

We received your delightful letter on returning from our holiday and thought the snaps were very good, especially the one of Cliff sitting at the edge of the pool. What a glorious pool that is. Like Cliff, if I were there, I should be in whenever the sun shone. You know, a private swimming pool has a psychological effect upon the ordinary Englishman and immediately conveys the impression of comparative wealth, the existence of which you have very kindly and tactfully suggested over a period of time both in your correspondence and photographs. The whole thing has its amusing side, inasmuch as when I first obtained an interview with those splendid Americans who were running the evacuation scheme at Grosvenor House, they impressed on me the intention of the Committee to place the children with families in America of about our own social and financial standing, the idea being that a child should not feel out of place either one way or the other. I can only think that I must have looked as if I had been left a lot of money – I certainly couldn't have looked intelligent enough to have made a pile myself. Grace suggests that I was gazing so fervently into the eyes of the lovely American lady by whom I was interviewed that she kept putting noughts on the end of the figure which I very truthfully gave her as my income. I say she stuck a nought on because she could see I was worth more than I was getting anyway.

Incomes in this country as you know are much lower per employed person than in America, and my own fifty to sixty dollars a week would be chicken feed to a man holding down the same job in your country. One does not as a rule discuss the subject of one's pittance and, by the way, I am working mine out on the basis of five dollars to the pound which of course is not the correct exchange rate at the moment. I am mentioning it to you because I cannot know whether you have gleaned a correct picture of our lives from Cliff's conversation, in which he might, from a sense of loyalty to us, have refrained from being completely outspoken, and as a result of this he might suffer embarrassment due to your not being aware of the standard of life to which he has been used in the past.

I feel that what I have said was perhaps quite unnecessary, but I shall never forget the three years I had after I went to sea. I got away as an engineer when I was seventeen by telling the marine superintendent that I was twenty-one, and for the rest of my experience with the company I had to be constantly on the alert against any question which might let the cat out of the bag. In later years I began to realise that the old marine super probably never swallowed my story, but preferred my audacity to my professed experience, although of course I had actually had three years' apprenticeship to engineering at that time, so I knew quite a bit about the job. However the fact remains that I was sailing under false colours as it were, and I should not care to have history repeat itself. Nuff said about that.

Will you please send a Flying Fortress or something similar over to transport us to that Utopian isle of yours. What a life, and your invitation to us to experience such a blissful existence is really appreciated, though to realise such a dream will necessitate one of those miracles the days of which some say are past. Also, will you please try to convey to your boys how much we appreciate their endeavours to improve our big son's skill in all the new games he is learning.

I must close down now. Cheerio until next time.

Bill Matthews to Grace and John Mathews

9 September 1941   Trelawny, Glendale, Ohio

In your last letter you devoted a paragraph to the matter of Cliff's environment as a guest in our household and quite frankly expressed a doubt that has, I take it, been growing in your minds concerning the promises made by the committees in London and New York that English children would be placed in similar environments when temporary homes were located for them in the USA. Janet and I are delighted with your frankness in bringing up any subject which may be a source of doubt or worry to you because we want to relieve you of anxieties concerning Cliff to the full extent of our combined abilities. I promise that we will be just as frank in return.

When we sent our application to New York requesting that we be allowed to care for an English child, I asked the local representative of the NY committee how complete a financial statement I should give in the blank space provided in the form. This man knew something of our financial status and replied that the applicants in our relative position in that regard were all putting in that space 'net worth more than $50,000'. Since I have promised to be frank, it is actually several times that figure. In this country we would be classified as 'people

The Matthews's house, Trelawny, 925 Congress Avenue, Glendale, Ohio.

The Matthews's backyard at Trelawny.

of means' but not really 'wealthy'. I did not think my statement in
the application meant very much because I knew we would later be
investigated (as we were) from several sources (banks, ministers)
before we would be approved or would have a child assigned to us.

Undoubtedly, Janet's reputation of being a most understanding
and unusual mother of boys and her obvious eagerness to have an
English child assigned to us had a great deal to do with our selection.
Also, I think Glendale is generally considered as a community where
parents live closely with their children and where family life is
perhaps a little more centered around the children than in some
other urban or suburban communities that I have known. At the
risk of boring you but at the same time continuing my promise to
be frank, I am going to give you some of our ideas on the subject of
privately accumulated wealth, its influence in our own family and
most important to you, of course, how it might influence Cliff, who
is temporarily a member of our family. I have said *our* ideas for
happily Janet and I are in complete accord on this subject, as we are
on most others for that matter. Our boys, as they mature and develop,
seem to be reasoning the thing out for themselves very much as
Janet and I would like to have them.

To me, privately accumulated wealth is just as dangerous as 'high
explosive'. So much depends upon what you do with it. What our

75

family has of it is mostly inherited and that is the dangerous kind. Fortunately our parents didn't pass on such deadly stuff without some pretty good instructions as to how to use it, and while I'm afraid we haven't done as good a job in handling it as we might have (it has softened us, I regret to say, just as it has a great many Americans) we did know better because we had been told. What we had been told was that this wealth was a trust for us to administer during our lives. I'm afraid as trustees we didn't perform very well from about 1925–30. However, I'm thankful to say that we have come to our senses and since 1931 we have been strong 'New Dealers', supporting reforms in the capitalist system which are necessary, we think, to save it and American Democracy. I hope it is not too late. We are supporting these reforms because as individual trustees we Americans are too unreliable. Our three boys are seeing the picture. Not much 'high explosive' will be passed on to them but they don't seem to mind a bit. When we get Hitlerism out of the way with youngsters like yours and ours coming along it ought to be quite a generation. The world needs them.

To return to the question of how our environment might influence Cliff. We do not live fashionably and we dislike being conspicuous and consequently are 'homebodies', with our principal social activities being with Glendale friends having similar simple tastes. We have, undoubtedly, too many possessions which are remnants of the past. Our house is larger than we would have it if it could be done over again now. It requires two servants, a laundress and a man on the place, which is about seven acres in size. The boys do not assist in its care, for most of the time we are here they are in school but in the summer at Pointe-au-Baril they do all the manual labor, at which Cliff assisted on the lighter jobs. We dislike special privileges that come with the false power created by wealth and our boys, who have always associated at public school with children of all groups social and financial, have not been considered 'set apart' or 'different' and therefore a natural congeniality with their associates was possible. In such surroundings we do not feel that Cliff will become 'high hat' or too much impressed with worldly goods.

That is the way we have planned it for our own children and we are following the same plan with Cliff because we felt that you would wish it. I hope if you had any doubts in this connection that they will now be removed.

Please do not get the impression that we consider ourselves 'pretty holy'. I'm afraid we have made and will make plenty of mistakes in bringing up children, but I honestly feel that handling the 'having-too-much-money' problem is not one of our major mistakes. ENOUGH OF THAT.

Janet handles the news so beautifully in her letters that I won't attempt to supplement. We in the USA are still going thru the pains of a democracy trying to become unified concerning what our part should be in this world conflict. It is puzzling and discouraging, but if it wasn't that way we wouldn't like it either for it would mean we didn't have even the fundamentals of a democracy.

Cliff still is suffering from hay fever as he probably will for the next few weeks until frost. On the advice of our doctor, Janet has secured a nasal filter which fits in each nostril without discomfort and it seems to help the irritation by keeping pollen from entering his nose. He is otherwise very well and behaves like the little gentleman that he is.

We are very glad that you had a nice holiday. I certainly hope that our two families may be permitted to have a holiday together sometime. We will have to work on that possibility as soon as this war is over.

With best wishes from all the 'Matthewses' of Glendale.

Janet Matthews to Grace and John Mathews

23 September 1941   Trelawny, Glendale, Ohio

Since Bill sent off a letter I have been letting the time slip by and suddenly realised today that I should get busy again.

Probably Cliff has told you the big news that our son 'B' is going to be married. It is rather a joke on Bill and me because we were married very young with a war hanging over our heads. But, somehow, we thought our boys would not do likewise. We are pleased that she is such a nice girl. With military training in the offing there was no chance of 'B' finishing his college education, so it seems to be the thing to do to be married and have a little time together. The girl's name is Mary Sather and I will send you a snapshot as soon as we have some. She comes from Iowa, which is an agricultural state, and is prepared to have her husband devote himself to farming and farm management. Also, she has had no luxuries to spoil her for living on his small earnings. The wedding is to be on 4 October and Cliff and Don are going out with us to it.

By taking a streamlined train we can go in twelve hours and the boys will only miss one day of school. I think it will be an interesting thing for Cliff to see that part of the country, especially as we have a little time in Chicago and it is one of our thriving cities. Don has never been out that way and is quite thrilled at the prospect.

Mrs Strohmenger called up to say that she had had a letter from you in which came the news that Mr Mathews had been sick. She wasn't quite definite about what the trouble was but I gather it was a matter of overdoing things. She seemed to think that a game of tennis was pretty dashing for such an old (!) man. I had to confess that Bill and I still indulge in a good bit of tennis and we are really old. I do hope that all is well by now and we are terribly sorry that anything in the way of illness had to come your way.

We have nothing but good news about Cliff. He has branched out in his friendships this fall. This afternoon there are twelve boys here playing football in the yard. The weather has been beautiful and every day after school he has been playing tennis with a variety of boys or having a go at football with the gang. School has started off well. We have told all the teachers to keep Cliff up to capacity. Last year they would not let us pile on the work because they felt he had an adjustment to make. This year they have no compunction.

Will you take any unfavourable report you may hear about Cliff's interest in his sisters with a grain of salt? He is really, we think, an unusually thoughtful brother. I think that the Strohmengers are so fond of the girls that they are not quite fair to Cliff. He writes letters, goes to see them and often telephones to find out how things are going. It is more difficult for the girls to come here as they must be driven and Cliff can ride his bicycle. This is not a complaint, but merely to put in a good word for your first-born who worries that you think he is not being nice enough to his sisters.

Don is back at his music, two band rehearsals, two orchestra rehearsals and two jazz band practices every week. It keeps him pretty busy with his work on the school paper and his lessons. We bought a couple of good symphonic Victrola records because we thought it would do us no harm to become more familiar with good music. Bill knows nothing about music and grows restless at a long concert, but he dutifully plays these records every few days and can now tell the difference between Beethoven's fifth and Dvorak's fifth. He goes about acquainting himself with music with the same drive as he goes about business.

Our St Bernard puppy grows daily more enormous and Bill says

Dave Peck, Don Matthews and Clifford in the pool.

he thinks they have sold us a cow instead of a dog. We try to keep him out of the house but he wedged his way in last night, knocked a vase of flowers off the table with one swish of his tail and then started to tear up a sofa pillow. We hope he will calm down with age.

By the time this reaches you I will be that old thing called a mother-in-law! Gosh, I hope I won't be the type you read about in jokes. It is going to be hard not to give out advice. So far, I have been nobly restrained but once or twice I have caught myself on the verge of offering unsolicited suggestions.

We all send our best to our English cousins.

John Mathews to Janet and Bill Matthews

25 September 1941

Hamilton, Hewarts Lane, Bognor Regis,
Sussex

We have received letter number two from the boss, but I must not begin to wax wildly appreciative or Mrs Matthews will give up writing in disgust and believe me we would rather go without our butter ration, which in peacetime would be equivalent to saying we would rather lose an arm or an eye. Suffice it to say that when deeply moved I become lost for words, and just now I am speechless. In future please refrain from writing letters so overflowing with kindness and goodwill; they bring tears to my eyes and that's pretty hard on a fellow who always had a reputation for being a cynical sort of bloke. I don't know whether it is the lack of vitamins, but I can't take it, so please be tough, tell us in our next letter that we are no good and never will be.

I am pleased to say that your ideas on the handling of wealth coincide with my own precisely, the only difference being that *you* have to worry about it. Be assured that from the time we received your first letters we were never worried about Cliff. He is an extraordinarily fortunate young fellow to be spending this phase of his life with you. We have never regarded ourselves as perfect parents and since the children left us we have realised the many things in that respect where we failed.

Nowadays the phrase which is repeated only too often in discussions is 'after the war is over', all too reminiscent of the speeches made during the last fracas, which were so conveniently forgotten afterwards. It is amazing how many people say to me, 'Oh well, we'll alter all that after the war,' but when I ask them how they propose to set about it the answer is almost without exception extremely vague and displays complete ignorance of the existing parliamentary system. This is because the poor fellow invariably left school at an early age, having received no education whatever in political matters either local or national. I myself left school at fourteen and was immediately apprenticed to engineering at a works about five miles from my home. I used to have to be up at 5 am in summer and 4.30 am in winter, when I had to catch the train instead of cycling in, and the hours were from 6 am to 6 pm. Shortly after joining the firm I was put on a fortnight of night work and a fortnight's day work, and before I was fifteen I was working all night on a lathe, turning out aeroplane strut ends in the last war. Food was short then, and I remember the horrible mess called sago pudding which I was given to eat after my sandwiches about 1 am. I usually spent the rest of my rest period boxing with my fellow apprentices. In summer I was ready for the whistle at 6 pm and was off on my bike like a shot, doing the five miles in about 12 minutes. I gulped my food, washed and changed, and was down on the tennis courts playing tennis until dark. Then Grace and I used to cycle to her home, have supper and it would be 11 pm before I could drag myself away from her. No wonder my long-suffering mother had such trouble rousing me next morning at 5 am. Strangely enough, I was always full of vim in those days and it was only when I started to run my own business and to worry that things changed.

I think there is little doubt that after this war the minimum school leaving age will be fixed at sixteen, and this will be a move in the right direction. Education must be the basis and starting of all reform. (I knew this letter was going to be a wow when I started out.) If there is anything you would like to have explained about this peculiar country and its people do ask in your letters. Our feelings will not be hurt. We are not touchy people.

Clifford with Janet Matthews.

Sheila riding, October 1942, a still from the home movie which the Strohmengers made and sent to John and Grace Mathews.

Another shot from the ciné film showing Dinah mounted behind Jean Strohmenger.

Sheila Mathews to her parents

17 October 1941   54 Forest Avenue, Wyoming, Ohio

We hope you heard our broadcast alright. The lady let us have much longer than any other children because they didn't have anything to say.

I just had a soda and I was thinking how much you would enjoy it if you could have one.

We all had our music lesson today. I had two pieces last week called 'Innocence' and 'Progress'. I have a new one this week which is a very pretty one, it is called 'The Clear Brook'.

We have started having fires now and it is quite cold.

We went riding the other day and our horses were very frisky and we started up a hill and they got into a gallop and suddenly my horse 'Nonsense' started bucking and shaking his head and I felt like I was in a rodeo. It was really fun having the wind blow in your face and going along so fast.

We are making a movie to send you of us riding so you will see how nice and fast we go.

Mr Betz our Social Science teacher showed us a movie of the inside of the White House and all President Roosevelt's things.

Give my love to Grandma and all the cousins. I hope you are all safe. It looks like the US will soon be in the war doesn't it?

Dear Josie
Thank you very much for your lovely letter, I enjoyed it immensely. Your sister is always thinking of you and hopes you are a big girl and help Mummy. I am so glad you don't cry when you fall down. Such a *big* girl.

Dinah, Gloria and Sheila, 1941

Sheila, Gloria and Dinah at the piano, 1941.

Don Matthews on the drums.

Clifford equipped for baseball.

Clifford taking aim with his air rifle.

Janet Matthews to Grace and John Mathews

December 1941   Trelawny, Glendale, Ohio

The pathetic picture you painted in your letter of the postman arriving without any American mail for the 'One Ts' has spurred me to immediate action. Your last letter was received here this morning looking like a lace doily. The censor has clipped big chunks out of the first page. We are left with the tantalising information that 'he and Winnie and his wife went off to London to shop.' Then a big hole until there is a mention of a bottle of whiskey. Of course, I am thinking the worst. You have obviously been 'hitting the bottle' along with the vitamins.

Naturally the biggest news for us as Americans is the war and our part in it. The bombing of Honolulu was a terrific shock. We have many friends on the islands because of a winter I spent there with the children when Bill was in the Orient. The civilian buildings are rather flimsy, most of the schools for instance being of the outdoor variety with just a roof overhead, so most of the bombs must have hit our Pearl Harbor base and airfields if only about one hundred civilian casualties occurred.

The news of the bombing came to us at the school, where we were having a Sunday afternoon rehearsal of our Stunt Night. As the performances are scheduled for Friday and Saturday of this week and considerable expense had been incurred for costumes, coach etc there seemed to be nothing to do but carry on. The money is to go to the United Service Organization, the agency which supplies our fighting forces with entertainment, writing paper, stamps and so on. When we started work on the performance the morale of our soldiers seemed a very acute problem, but now that we are at war morale will be automatically improved. It was the feeling of training for

Clifford taking part in a broadcast to Britain, 21 December 1941. Mrs Dawn Clark, who represented the United States Committee for the Care of Evacuee Children, is at the table.

what appeared to the boys as an unnecessary precaution that made them restless.

There wasn't a person of the hundred or so rehearsing who did not want to go home and listen to the radio, but not one soul left and we went on as if nothing had happened. Many of the news commentators have said in the last few days that they have been struck by the similarity in the way the British and the Americans have taken the news of actual war. There is no excitement, remarkably little hate, just a sort of quiet and grim determination to go through with it. There are certain advantages. The isolationists will be silenced.

Everyone wants something to do and I hope they will not coddle us but will give us all jobs and demand sacrifices from us at once.

As to our own family, it means of course the older boys must go and I don't feel very brave about that. We have brought them up to think that war is the most foolish and unprofitable thing in the world. We have been worried for fear we had so thoroughly imbued them with pacifistic ideas that they would be unhappy if they had to fight. However, Bill had a talk with 'B' recently in which 'B' said that he had been doing a lot of thinking of late and had decided that there is a point at which you realise that it is necessary to fight for the things you believe in.

Enough of that. School reports are in today. We are proud of both boys as they have shown improvement all along the line. We have had fun kidding Cliff because American History is his poorest subject. He had to start from scratch to learn about the Yankees.

Please excuse the unusually large number of mistakes. I am very tired. The last few days have been rather nerve-racking and we have had the rehearsing to make it worse. At least I am getting a lot of knitting done while waiting my cue. I am at present making a sweater for a man who must have taken vitamins from birth. Why are all Red Cross sweaters so enormous? I made this one for a man who was huge in body but with a withered arm, the result of doing one sleeve in the dark at a night rehearsal. I suppose it will have to be done again as the Red Cross never seem to take into account that all men are not physically perfect.

John Mathews to Jean and Warren Strohmenger

Hamilton, Hewarts Lane, Bognor Regis,
28 December 1941   Sussex

I hope you got my cable saying that we had heard the broadcast because it was absolutely tip top. It is a great compliment to you that the girls came over so well, we could detect no sign of nerves or hesitation. We were delighted to hear Gloria's voice. She sounded so affectionate with her, 'Hello Uncle Jack, Auntie Grace and Jo.'

We used our own set to get the broadcast and were almost shivering with fright when we found we were tuned to Schenectady instead of Cincinnati, but I immediately found the right station and we breathed again. Sheila's piano playing sounded as though she might have been in the same room. My heart was in my mouth when she faltered about half way through, but she struggled bravely on and I think she deserves a medal both for her playing and her pluck, as there cannot be many children her age who have broadcast pianoforte music. Dinah seems to have gone right ahead with her reading, as I presume she was reading from your prepared script. We thought she was lucky to have someone to type hers out when we heard one of the other girls trying to read from longhand. Thank you very much for the treat. It made our Christmas much happier than it might have been.

After that the film arrived safely and completed our pleasure over the holiday. I eventually managed to hire a projector and screen, and the film was shown after tea on Xmas evening to an audience of seventeen. I had never used a projector before but I had a private tryout and then ran it through three times on the night. You should have heard the children scream with delight when they recognised their cousins. We recognised you, Jean, using the typewriter and especially enjoyed the bit where Warren got all tied up with the presents at the birthday party. I have shown the film fifteen times now and kept the projector a week, but however much they sting me for the rental it will be worth it to have seen a filmed record of our children's stay in America.

I have not returned to work yet after my illness but expect to shortly. The experts I saw in Southampton reported no organic trouble. I told them my own impression was that I had a touch of nervous exhaustion, and they seemed inclined to agree. I feel a lot stronger and the feeling of depression I had has practically

Bill and Harry Matthews with Barry the dog.

disappeared. I feel like a smoke again and I can take a glass of beer with a certain amount of pleasure, and that must be a good sign.

We have been puzzling over your description of Dinah's nervousness lately. It certainly is a change from her behaviour at home. I used to get her standing on my shoulders and she would fall forward with me holding on to her ankles without fear. I wonder if it is a reaction to the gunfire and general noise of air raids which she experienced before she left. I hope she grows out of it. The effect of bombing on young children over here has received a good deal of attention, and it is found that they display extreme fear at the most simple things such as walking along a plank only a foot from the floor or climbing a tiny step ladder. In the special nurseries which are set aside for them they are given treatment which gradually diminishes their fear and enables them to regain their self-confidence.

We all send our best wishes for a happy and victorious New Year. By the way, Jo cried when she saw the film because she said the girls didn't see her. I suppose she thought they ought to have waved to her.

Grace Mathews to Janet and Bill Matthews

3 February 1942   Hamilton, Hewarts Lane, Bognor Regis, Sussex

I think it is quite time I endeavoured to write you another letter. The mails have not been arriving so well lately but I suppose we must expect that now you are in this war. I am so sorry, I had hoped that American mothers would be spared that. Among the minor inconveniences, you are already rationed for sugar, I read, and by yesterday's paper it may soon include clothing. We find that menfolk do not notice it so much as women and growing children. I find it very difficult with Josie. We have been particularly badly hit because, living in rooms as we are now doing, I have not kept as many things as I would had we been in our home, and it is surprising how useful once discarded clothes are becoming.

I expect you are also feeling the effects of your busy time through Christmas. How I envy the Americans' vitality. You seem to get so much into one day. I think travelling facilities help you. It seems now that I spend more than half the day walking to and fro. We live half-an-hour's walk from the shops, which we have to visit every day, for if we can't get our half a pound of biscuits one day we may the next. The buses run every half hour but they are so crowded, and more than enough children around here have whooping cough. The mothers still take them on the buses, which is very wrong. I suppose Josie will have it one day but I don't like running into it.

I wonder if you, like us, are having a very severe winter. We awoke

Harry Matthews sets off for college again.
Left to right: Betty, Harry, Janet, Don, Mary and 'B'.

yesterday to find another fall of snow. Luckily the rain came and washed it away. Usually, before the thaw has been complete, we have had another frost, leaving us with about two inches of ice on the road. You can guess the state we are in with not enough labour to clear the roads apart from the main streets. Oh, for the land of peace and sunshine. We picked up a Canadian soldier when we were with Jack in the car recently. He said he came from the Niagara Falls district where he could go out of his back door and pick a peach when he wanted it. Apparently they also had snow but with bright sunshine. He didn't like our kind.

Your mention of Cliff's banana sandwich brought back memories. Josie is very curious about bananas. She has a lot of treats to come after the war, we tell her.

The cold weather has been very trying to Jack but he has done his best to carry on. Unfortunately he has had a lot of trouble with his office staff. One young female after another has taken it into her head that the war work she was doing at the Petroleum Board was not sufficient and has decided that having a family would be more patriotic.

It was simply grand hearing our own children's voices last time they broadcast, and such a surprise to hear Harry. I have my own picture of what he is like and I am sure it is right. Perhaps next time we shall be able to hear Don. Why can't we finish off this fight? Think of the lovely time we will have when we meet. I admit I'm generally as poor a conversationalist as letter writer, but won't I talk. I am usually shy, but I think there will be too much to say for that.

You can guess how terribly we miss the children and when I hear their voices I long for just a second to give them a great big hug, yes, Cliff included, though I think I shall have to reach up to him if he goes on growing. But it is our comfort that they are so well cared for and so happy.

We have had here this week a waste-paper salvage campaign. It is surprising what people have managed to turn out. They even beg for old love letters to be sacrificed. What price victory, not a love letter left. But one little word – they are not getting our American ones.

Well, it is now time for John to come to lunch and Josie is worrying to write her line of kisses for you, so I must conclude though I know this is not half as long as your letters.

Clifford Mathews to his parents

29 March 1942   766 Bay Esplanade, Clearwater, Florida

Well, we have arrived in Florida and we are having wonderful weather. I have quite a tan already.

We had a keen trip down here. We got up at about 6 am and went down to the Cincinnati terminal. It is a beautiful station with huge murals around the walls depicting work that is done in the city. Cincy by the way is quite famous for its machine tool factories. From the station I called Sheila to say goodbye. We got on the train and ate breakfast while we crossed the Ohio river and went into Kentucky. It is pretty mountainous and the scenery is wonderful. As we went further south the trees started to turn green and I saw an occasional daffodil. On into Tennessee we went and then ate lunch. The meals on these trains are prepared and served by negroes and are very good. The soil began to turn red as we went south. We were soon into Georgia and after dinner and some cards went to bed. I was sleeping in a lower bunk and so could look at the stars and the light from an occasional cabin by the railroad.

I woke up about 4.30 and just lay in bed and watched the sun come up and the Floridians get up and start their day's work. We arrived at Clearwater at about 8.30, where Clyde the Matthews's chauffeur was waiting for us. After breakfast I walked around the gardens where such things as oranges, grapefruit and papayas grow. When we want orange juice or a grapefruit we just go out and pick one, it's marvellous.

I hope you got the cable we sent for Daddy's birthday.

As I write this there are three heavy bombers in the air patrolling over here. They are huge Flying Fortresses, B-17Es to be exact, and they really make a racket when they come down low. I saw a Lockheed Hudson with RAF insignia yesterday.

I have been fishing with two boys from Glendale who are down here. They are Bill Burchenal and Tom Carruthers. We went along the beach to the end of the island and there cast our lines off from the groin. Tom caught two fair-sized sheepheads and I got a nice flounder. Poor Bill got nothing more than a good burn. We went to the yacht club for dinner that evening and the sunburn hurt him so much that he had to leave in the middle of it.

I hope to have some photos for you next letter.

Jean Strohmenger to Grace and John Mathews

22 June 1942   54 Forest Avenue, Wyoming, Ohio

Warren is waiting to take this letter, one to my folks and his great big envelope – addressed to the Navy Department, The Office of Naval Officer Procurement – to the post office and get them all into the mail. Warren is now a lieutenant in the US Navy, so I wanted to get this letter off to you to tell you that the time has come, and that we would appreciate you sending the money to help out a little bit with the girls. We have talked it over and tried to decide whether we should try to keep them at all, but I do hate to have them buffeted around, and they have made all the adjustments here and are used to the school and us and have a lot of little friends in the neighbourhood with whom they can play and have lots of fun. There is not going to be as much money to spend when Warren goes, but we are all pretty well supplied with clothes so we'll just have to get along the best we can. I don't believe the war is going to last as long again as it has already, so if the United Nations can ever get started

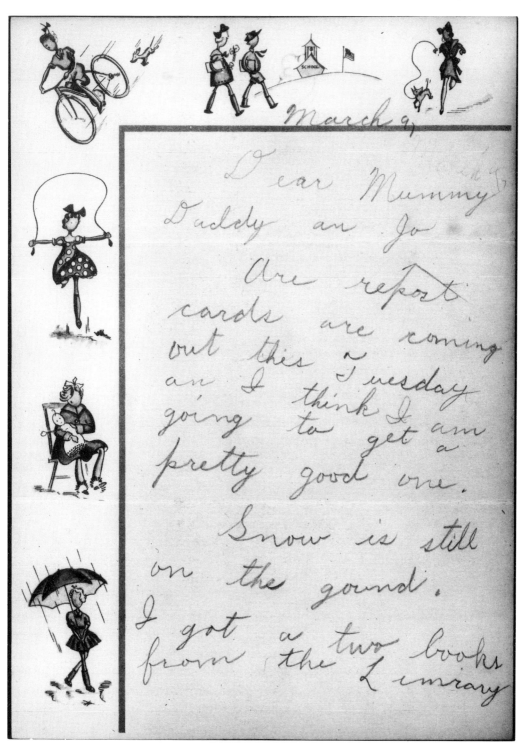

March 9,

Dear Mummy
Daddy an Jo

Are report
cards are coming
out this Tuesday
an I think I am
going to get a
pretty good one.

Snow is still
on the gound.
I got a two books
from the Library

A letter from Dinah.

The Strohmengers and Sheila and Dinah on horseback, 1941.

rolling (and, of course, they will now that Warren will be in it) it won't be long now. We have to get Warren's office closed up, all the patients notified and then all the office furniture stored.

It is rather hard to give up all this nice practice that he has spent ten years building up but, after all, if we don't get Hitler and Hirohito stopped his practice won't be worth much anyway and, too, the fellows in the fighting lines need some good doctors to take care of them, eh what? . . .

We'll have to get over to the Post Office so I'd better close. I hate to have to tell you to send the money, but I suppose you would rather do that than have the girls sent some place else. I don't even know if they would be able to get a home here in this city because now that we are in the war too I'm afraid folks won't be as willing to take on added responsibilities. We realise that you won't be able to send enough to keep them, but every little bit will help and we'll try to make the best of it.

Janet Matthews to Grace and John Mathews

26 June 1942   Trelawny, Glendale, Ohio

Your last letter distinguished itself by making excellent time. It was postmarked 15 June in England and we had it served with our breakfast on 26 June. We were sorry to hear that John will have to have an operation on his nose and highly sympathetic as all the Matthews are 'nosey'. That high pulse rate must be disturbing for an energetic man. Do not worry about what sort of shape you are in when we see you after the war. In the proposed international tennis match between the One and Two Ts when it is all over, it is more than likely it will be the Two Ts who will fall to pieces.

I had a strenuous experience this week and it made me feel very old. In an unguarded moment I told a young college boy, who is interested in ornithology, that I should like to go with him on a bird walk to learn more about our birds. We were to meet at 6.15 *am* but I overslept and had to go without breakfast. We went to a wooded hillside and scrambled up and down, through blackberry thickets, fording swollen streams until I was thoroughly scratched and my feet were soaking wet. It seems that we were searching for a VERY shy bird called a 'chat'. It is the largest of the warblers and we could hear the call of the pesky little fellows but they were coy about coming out in the open. Now I truly love birds but it seems to me that if they want privacy the only decent thing to do is let them have it. After any number of trips up and down hill, a mocking bird sang out at the top and of course we were at that time at the bottom. It was bitter to make the climb again as I can see a mocking bird by merely walking out of the house in Florida, so I suggested that I stay down and perhaps surprise the chat. While my guide was gone I sat down and took about a ton of mud off my shoes and squeezed water out of the bottom of my slacks and thought of breakfast. We got home at nine-thirty and I was almost too tired to eat. All day I was dull at my work and ever since I have had a lame foot. So you see what a spry young thing you will be up against here.

We have great news from 'B' and Mary. They are expecting a baby in October. Mary has been wretched for several months and is nervous because her mother died when a younger brother of Mary's was born. Mary has a very nice step-mother but far away in Iowa and we feel very responsible for her wellbeing. She looked so pale and thin the last time she was here that Bill called the doctor to ask if all was well. He said he thought so but that she was having an unusual amount of nausea. Poor little thing, she seems so young. We are now called Grandma and Grandpa by our friends, which is not calculated to make you feel like a spring chicken.

Don has taken a job at the dairy farm in Glendale and rides his bicycle back and forth to work and carries his lunch with him. He is in the room where they bottle the milk and they sterilise with steam. The first day he went it was a very hot day and I gather he felt a little faint from the terrific heat, but he seems to be getting used to it. He is dog-tired when he comes home and two nights a week he takes typing lessons. It is a strenuous regime for a boy his age but he is strong and happy to be busy.

Did I tell you that Don had won the music award at school this year? I think it is for the most outstanding pupil. I did not go to the try-outs but I was told that he gave a history of drumming from the earliest days and illustrated it with various drum rhythms, ending up with a rip-snorting example of modern jazz rhythm. I think I was even more thrilled than he was because I know that it has not been easy during all those years of being the youngest brother and he needs a little confidence.

Do you talk much in England about stamping out all race prejudice? It is interesting here to see how much it is being discussed. The South still believes that the negro should be kept in his place and by that they mean in a position of inferiority, not properly educated, kept from voting and, above all, segregated. While the northern states have always been more liberal they haven't done much about it. Now, since we have so many colored troops and allies of all races, there is a definite campaign to impress upon us the fact that our constitution says that all men are created equal. It is a subject that Bill and I feel very strongly about and we are delighted to notice a more liberal and broadminded trend.

Next week there is to be a big benefit performance for the families of our soldiers and sailors. There are to be two ball games and some sort of mock battle enacted by soldiers. It is in the evening and Cliff, Don, Bill and I are going. I hate to think of the difficulty we shall have parking the car. Bill is the sort of person who is always late everywhere. I like to see the curtain go up at the theatre or the first ball pitched at a ball game. What usually happens is that we leave for the game late. We arrive so near to the ball park that we can hear the people shouting. I wonder what is going on, but not Bill. He is going to find just the right place to park the car if it takes all night.

We pass parking lot after parking lot, but none looks just right. Either the parking attendant looks like just the sort of guy who would mash your fenders as soon as you left the car or he has the wrong-coloured eyes. Finally a suitable lot is found but do we get out and let the man park the car? You know we don't. We back and shunt, we argue as to whether someone will block us in, which is a waste of breath as we are obviously the last people to arrive at the game. Of course, the lot is miles from the ball park and there is a wild sprint to get there. The shouts from the spectators within indicate great excitement and we finally arrive at the park. Do we seek our seats? No, we must have a program so that we will be able to tell if some very obscure player is called into the game. Bill knows all the regulars by sight. That takes another five minutes and we finally settle into our seats when only about a third of the game is over.

Now I work it like this. I leave for the game late, not because I am busy like Bill but because I am a bad manager. I arrive near the park. I see a dirty little urchin who will take care of my car for a quarter. I leave the car. I run for the game, not stopping to buy a program. The game is well under way and there are a number of strange men playing. I wish I had a program to find out who they are. After the game I seek my car. There are at least six cars between me and the exit, or once, even worse, there was a big policeman who said, 'Is this your car, lady?' I said it was and almost added that I thought it was a pretty car, but he looked stern and said that it was parked by a fire hydrant and that it would cost me a two dollar fine. I remonstrated and said that I had been led to that spot by a nice little boy, but he was of the opinion that I was old enough to recognise a fire hydrant for myself and if I didn't care to pay the fine then and there I could go to court, where it would probably cost me five or six dollars. I paid the two.

Maybe Bill is smarter than I am after all. It would be terrible to marry someone who was just like yourself, there would be nothing to laugh at and heaven knows that a laugh is worth a lot these days.

I feel that this letter is all about us and not much about Cliff in whom you are naturally most interested, but I know that he wrote to you today and I do not want to repeat all his news. When the sun shines again we will take a picture of him and send it to you, but we must have set some kind of record for rain during this month of June. He looks pretty tall these days and I cannot pat him on the top of the head without reaching up, not that I would attempt such a thing now he has grown such a man. It is only raining a little just now so I will get on my bicycle and take this to the post office. We send our love and hope this finds you well, as the Southerners say.

John Mathews to Jean and Warren Strohmenger

5 July 1942   Hamilton, Hewarts Lane, Bognor Regis, Sussex

We have just received your letter giving us the news about Warren becoming a naval lieutenant and I am writing by return to tell you that I have written today for an application form to send the £6 a month off each month, and will make the necessary arrangements with the bank to transfer the money immediately I get the okay from London.

Congratulations, Warren, on the commission and our sympathy on having to give up a splendid practice. Let's hope all your patients can survive until you get back, and when you do they will all flock back to you with added numbers, I'm certain. You must be sure to return as an admiral at least. Of course, our first thought when we heard the news was whether you will get as far as England and, if you do, we expect a wire from you right away – and how we shall look forward to seeing you.

Going back to the money question, we would send more if we could but that is the maximum they will allow. However every little helps, and we can only hope that it will make it possible for you to keep the children with you, but as I have said before you must consider your own welfare first now. Although it would be tough for the kids to have to move, you must let me know without hesitation if keeping them is going to be too inconvenient and I will then apply to the Evacuation Committee to find other accommodation for them. They are young and would have to adjust themselves. Don't think for a moment that we like the idea by any means, but you took them when there was little idea of America coming into this war and it would be most unfair if, as a result of your goodness of heart then, you should suffer now. We cannot know the position in which you find yourselves, and we can only leave it to you to do what you think is best for all.

As you say, the war cannot possibly last long now that Warren is in it. I looked in the paper this morning to see if Hitler had cried off, but he apparently hadn't heard the news yet. Well, he's got it coming to him now. Oh heck, I wish I could get into this business myself. I'm going to feel pretty cheap when my grandchildren ask, 'What did you do in the Great War, Grandpa?'

I must apologise, I had been thinking all the week about sending off a cable to you for Independence Day and then on the day I was so darned busy I forgot all about it until the evening, and then the post office was closed. I cussed until I was blue in the face and cussed Grace for not reminding me. One of your army boys celebrated the day by taking a bet from a pal that he would not jump off London Bridge. He handed his coat to his friend and jumped off the parapet and swam ashore. He then rejoined his friends on the bridge, collected his bet and went off in a taxi to change his clothes. We'll see that Warren does not do anything like that if he comes over.

We shall look forward to your next letter and hope that things will pan out as you would wish.

I want to send this up to the post by one of the office girls who is going with the depot mail, so will get this away now.

Love to you all from Grace and Jo, and give all three of the girls a kiss from me.

John Mathews to Janet and Bill Matthews

16 July 1942   Hamilton, Hewarts Lane, Bognor Regis, Sussex

I had some difficulty starting this letter. As soon as I had typed 'Dear' the letter 'D' came unstuck from my typewriter, so I had to get the soldering iron out and repair it. Save all your old kettles for after the war and I'll mend them for you. I'm the cat's whiskers with a soldering iron and that's an Englishman's understatement. The saving of scrap of all sorts is an old story to us over here. In fact there is practically no scrap from the kitchen. Any meat that we get is boned, and we have a way of looking rather askance at anyone leaving anything uneaten from their portion. The only thing I remember us wasting in the last year was a small cake which looked in the window a rather tasty chocolate sponge confection but, when we attempted to eat it, was a whitened sepulchre. Grace dutifully placed it before us at tea three days running but Jo and I refused to acknowledge its presence, so she attempted to turn it into a sponge pudding with ersatz custard. Oh boy, it was like trying to eat rubber. One must be careful not to throw away anything such as paper or string. In fact, if one is seen throwing away a cigarette carton in the street one is likely to end up before the judge. They are pretty strict about that sort of thing, and rightly so.

One of the things which has become very popular over here because of the rationing is the second-hand clothes market. In some of the ladies' journals, especially one called *The Lady,* there are always hundreds of ads for costumes, frocks, shoes, hats and the rest. As I write this, Grace is studying it carefully. Apparently there is a black crocodile handbag advertised for eight guineas – about forty-five dollars. I do not even raise an eyebrow. Now she mentions a 'nice sounding' costume of turquoise blue with all the trimmings at twelve-and-a-half guineas, or sixty dollars to you. The swindle is that you can buy all these second-hand things without giving up your coupons, with the result that if you have a good costume that you are tired of you can easily get more than you paid for it new by selling it in this way. If you want to buy, you have to be jolly quick off the mark because each ad is answered by dozens of applications. You can understand this when you realise that we get twenty coupons over a period of nine months and a new costume, tailor or readymade, takes eighteen. A suit for me took, I believe, 26 coupons, a sweater five, so men's second-hand clothes are also in very good demand.

We go to tremendous lengths to preserve them. In the case of a sports jacket (dark green) of mine, when the elbows and cuffs became frayed I went to a garage friend and he let me have some green motor car upholstery taken from an old wreck. It was quite good leather and I could not buy new stuff of course. I took it to the tailor with the jacket and he sewed in a large piece round each elbow and narrow strips round the cuffs and, hey presto, I have a new jacket. I have three pairs of flannel pants, two with the seats worn through, but I insist on wearing them on fire watch at the depot and the landlady's daughter here, Winnie, has a good laugh at me when I go off in my holey pants. Clothing coupons, by the way, are not only for clothes, one has to buy towels, face flannels etc with them as well. I tell you all this so that when you arrive at the dockside after the war and see a tramp trying to hold his pants up with one hand and wave his crownless hat with the other you'll know it is me.

No, we don't talk a lot in this country about race prejudice, at

John Mathews typing one of his letters in the garden at Hamilton.

least not in peacetime. Just at the moment, of course, there is a race of people for whom we have a slight antipathy shall I say, but the negro doesn't appear in our problems because he is almost non-existent over here – I have not seen one for weeks. I cannot say just how we should feel about them if the situation were the same in this country as in yours. From what I remember of history, it is entirely our fault that you have the problem today. As an outsider, I should say that if the negro pays taxes equivalent to the white, he should have access to the same educational facilities and the right to vote.

I can see that the question of segregation is a very thorny one, but on thinking it over it does seem to me that there is a link with education, and I do not mean education limited to the three 'Rs'. For example, I have been sitting on deck during my days at sea talking to an Indian stevedore and suddenly the latter, who has been chewing betel nut, has spat a stream of blood red saliva on to the deck. At that point, my desire for segregation has been immediate and profound. On the other hand, an educated Indian has nothing to learn from us and I presume the same applies to the negro. Frankly, though, I do not think I should care to work under a negro boss, so you see I haven't the courage of my own convictions.

Did I ever tell you I miss Cliff pretty badly at times? Most unEnglish of me probably but I do. I was in the car today and through some trees I saw white flannel trousers so, sensing a cricket match, I got out to have a look. There were two teams of schoolboys all dressed in their flannels and white shirts and school caps playing cricket in the sunshine with two schoolmasters as umpires. It looked good, and I could picture Cliff playing there had he been over here. When you come over, I must take you to see Winchester playing another college side on a sunny day. Even if you knew nothing of the game you would be bound to appreciate the beauty of the scene. Well, that's enough sentimental nonsense for one innings.

I was on fire watch last night, so now I go to bed.

John Mathews to Janet and Bill Matthews

25 August 1942   Hamilton, Hewarts Lane, Bognor Regis, Sussex

We have not had a letter from Wyoming for over six weeks. My guess is that Mrs S has decided that the situation calls for every possible economy and she has decided to send all her mail by boat, with the result that Davy Jones has received some of the mail addressed to us.

I was supposed to have been in hospital last weekend, but owing to the raid on Dieppe[1] I cancelled it for a week and I go up this Friday. I did so because although we were told it was a raid I had a feeling that it was the beginning of the invasion proper, and I felt I ought to be on the job. When we heard that the troops were returning I was quite disappointed. It was a busy time anyway and quite exciting because there was one continual air raid warning and Jerry

---

[1] A force of some 6,000 men, which consisted largely of Canadian troops, landed at Dieppe on 19 August 1942. The raiders were unable to capture the town and after nine hours of fighting withdrew as planned. More than half of the Canadians were killed or taken prisoner in one of the most costly single operations of the war.

flew in occasionally and dropped a few bombs not far away. It was very low cloud in the evening and one of them flew just over our house. During the night following, the sky was lit up with flares and terrific flak. The flares seem to be hanging on sky hooks, they take so long to come down, and dozens of Bofors open up at them with tracer shells. It really looks like a first class fireworks display. We have no air raid shelter in our part of the house, and we were having tea when one Jerry flew over just prior to dropping a couple. You should have seen Grace and Jo dive under the table. It is not much use sheltering under a table, of course, but you get an urge to duck under anything handy and then laugh at yourself when you come out. You would be tickled to hear Jo say in a very offhand manner as the siren goes, 'Warning,' just as she might say, 'It's raining'. I suppose it seems completely natural to her as she has heard it during most of her life so far.

I have enclosed a cutting from our newspaper to show that your boys can get along over here, but there are snags still and one that seems to be insoluble without a good deal of cheery common sense on both sides is the fact that your fellows are so much better paid than ours. Grace and I had a very amusing conversation with two of our own fighter pilots a day or so ago. One of them mentioned that a pilot of equivalent rank to his own gets about four times as much pay. He told us that he was in a pub recently when a boy from the USAAF came in, plonked £4 on the bar and requested the landlord to keep filling the glasses of everyone present until the money was gone. The English boy said with a grin on his face, 'I don't mind telling you, I did my best in the time available,' but, as he commented, it can be rather irksome when hunting through one's pocket for a last half crown to see a fellow come in with a fistful of notes and start throwing money about *ad lib*. I was very pleased to hear them say, however, that they both realised that the Yank (do Americans object to being called Yanks or Yankees, by the way?) was simply trying to be friendly. They blamed the system that paid them so little and did not begrudge the other fellow his good luck and I entirely agree with them. Why the fighting man should be paid less than the munition worker has always defeated me. If we can afford to fight, surely we ought to pay the fighters the most money.

Grace and I were lucky again the other day. A Hun came over and did his usual machine gun stunt and dropped a stick of heavy ones on the town. We had passed the spot where one dropped only a few minutes before. The ceiling of our favourite cinema came down during the raid but the manager told us there wasn't the slightest panic. It was not heavy of course as I believe they make them of papier mâché. Grace, Jo and I had to go to another cinema the following afternoon about a hundred yards away and during the show a notice was put on the screen to say that an air raid warning had sounded. Not a soul left their seats (grammar?) despite the previous afternoon's shake up. Two Canadian soldiers a few seats from us slept through the whole thing. Which goes to show that we must all be completely daffy, or else that people can get used to almost anything. By the way, you may get the idea that we are frightful people taking Jo into a place of danger like that, but she is as safe there as at home and we would rather have her with us at such times than with anyone else.

Is 'B' really going to enlist and what will he go for, the navy? I seem to imagine him there. What a strange world we live in today. We little thought when Cliff went to you that we should later be talking of your own boy joining up.

I must get my toothbrush and razor together for my trip up to town tomorrow.

Jean Strohmenger to Grace and John Mathews

26 October 1942   54 Forest Avenue, Wyoming, Ohio

Your letter and snapshots arrived three or four days ago. Jo is getting quite tall we noticed and your other two girls are doing likewise if letting down hems makes me the judge.

It seems definite now that we are going to go to Peru, Indiana, to be nearer to Warren. The girls have a holiday this Friday so we are driving up there for the weekend. We won't be able to do that after the last of November when gas rationing starts so while we are there we will make some arrangements and then probably move up to live there in a week or two.

We drove up to Kokomo a month ago and stayed in an apartment that Warren had taken over in the hope that we would settle there, but the apartment was about as bad as the hotel we tried on an earlier visit. It was quite nicely furnished but only one square away from the Pennsylvania railroad depot and right on the main highway from Indianapolis going north. On top of that there was a Catholic church with a bell that started at 5 am and continued on from there. Peru is a smaller town than Kokomo so I hope it may be a little quieter, and it is only six miles from the base. We will have to take our furniture but the navy will move it for us.

The girls are quite frank about it. They don't want to go, especially Sheila and Dinah. Gloria has never moved in her life, so she is game for a change. It does make us feel good that the girls like their home here and that the school has been so enjoyable. Compliments are rather few and far between and everything is taken pretty much for granted, so we have to get our satisfaction out of little remarks like that. It really is Warren who is most anxious for us to come up. I went through all my agony before he left for the navy. I really was getting quite an inferiority complex because he seemed so anxious to go and I thought he didn't care anything about his home at all. However, after he had been there about two weeks things began to change, and just when I was beginning to get pretty well adjusted at home Warren starts tuning up. He is the determined type who keeps after us until he has his way. Maybe the change will be good for all of us but I am sorry we are going up this weekend because Saturday is Hallowe'en (the second anniversary of the girls' coming to our home) and all the children have such a good time in their costumes and going around to all the homes, but we have to get this business settled before Warren and I are both nervous wrecks.

It is about time for the girls to be coming home from school. Sheila usually waits for the other two and they come home together. Dinah has her own bicycle now, a hand-me-down from the folks across the street which we fixed up for her. Gloria and Sheila both ride Gloria's which has a back seat. There are twelve children on bikes who start down the street together in the morning now, so you see the gas rationing is having its effect already. The only bad thing is that they had to come home in the rain two days this week. However, we got their things right off and hung up to dry, and maybe they will be hardened a little by the exposure.

I'm afraid Warren is going to suffer for this letter to you. I don't think I'll be so ambitious about writing much to him tonight. I can't afford to let him down, though, because he has been writing like sixty ever since he arrived in Peru.

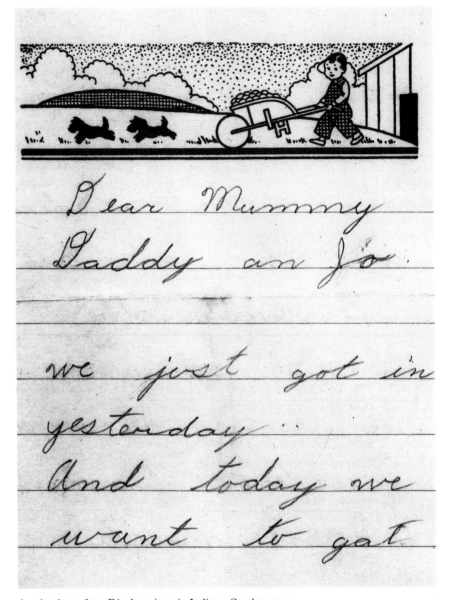

Dear Mummy
Daddy an Jo.

we just got in
yesterday
And today we
want to gat

Another letter from Dinah, written in Indiana, October 1942.

John Mathews to Janet and Bill Matthews

Hamilton, Hewarts Lane, Bognor Regis,
17 December 1942   Sussex

We are having to spend our Xmas here at Hamilton. I managed to get a whole heap of holly today with a lovely lot of berries on it and have decorated the dining room this evening. All our streamers and candle holders and whatnot are at our previous residence, the bungalow at Michelmersh where we stayed a month or so before coming here. Turkeys or chickens are almost impossible to obtain. Our grocer has fifteen tinned turkeys to share between over two hundred customers, so he says he is going to put all the names in a hat and the lucky ones will draw a turkey. We have about a thirteen to one chance – you never know your luck! If we don't get one we intend to beg, borrow or steal a tame rabbit, which can be almost as nice as chicken anyway, and Grace has managed to get a small tinned Xmas pudding into which we shall stick a sprig of holly and pour over it a quarter of an inch of brandy which Winnie has saved in the bottom of a bottle. So you can think of us gorging ourselves. The question of Xmas presents has been plenty tough. The few toys in the shops are absolute trash and a terrific price, so I decided to make Jo a modern-style settee and two armchairs for her doll's house. Grace is sitting in front of me now covering them with some odd pieces of taffeta silk and they are beginning to look absolutely tip top, or keen, as Cliff would say.

Grace has been worrying me lately to buy her a second-hand cycle because it is so difficult getting to the shops and back before Jo has to be collected from school. I've pretended to be either completely uninterested or against the proposition and for the last few days she seems to have given it up as a bad job. New bicycles are practically unobtainable, but I have a friend in the business at Midhurst and he has obtained a new Raleigh for me. I am having a blind man make a basket seat for the back so that she can take Jo to school on it and then go on and do her shopping. I am going to have some job getting it into the house without her knowing, but it will be worth it because I am sure she is going to have a happy day when she gets her cycle. She has not ridden one for years and I can imagine it will be rather nice to start again. I shall have to get one myself and then we can rediscover the byways together. I don't know what I have coming to me, but Win (our landlady's daughter) and Grace went up to

London a week ago and I have a sneaking idea that they managed to buy me about the last silk tie in the country, so it looks as though I shall be in luck myself on Christmas morning.

The radio gave out today that two raiders were shot down over the South and South East coast, so there is no secret in it. I saw one after the crash, and after he had dropped his bombs. You never saw such a mess in your life – it was just a lot of small pieces spread all over the place – and you can guess what happened to the crew. Considering they had just been gunning down any civilians they could see, they had it coming to them. I see it also says in the press that our gasometer was hit, so there is also no secret in that. Do you have gas cookers or do you not use such antiquated methods? We shall cook our Xmas dinner if I have to build a mud oven on the lawn.

I'm afraid this is a short letter, but I have 49,000 letters and Xmas cards to get off, so as time presses I must get down to it.

Janet Matthews to Grace and John Mathews

25 January 1943   Trelawny, Glendale, Ohio

This letter should begin with an apology. You have been badly neglected but really through no fault of mine. A very sad thing happened. I had word that my mother had died and we had to go east to the funeral and to arrange about the disposal of her possessions. Naturally it was a great blow. While I am quite sure that life had long since become a burden to her, because of ill health and the loss of her hearing and the failing of her sight, she was a gallant little person and managed to take an interest in the doings of her family. I hope that I shall be able to show such courage in the face of any adversity that may strike me.

Usually I am so disgusted with my letters that I never want to see them again, but I wish I had a carbon of my last effort so that I could refresh my memory about what news was sent your way. I hope there will not be too much repetition.

I don't think I told you that Harry has left for training in the Coast Guard. He is at a large base near New York. When he left here he was selected to take charge of the group and we thought that was a fine start and that he looked like an admiral. Of course, it meant nothing but we were pleased anyway. When we were in the

GLENDALE MONITOR

Vol. III - No. 4   GLENDALE, OHIO   January, 1943

The masthead of Clifford's school newspaper.

east we were allowed to go out and see him for about an hour. He looked in the pink of condition and seemed very pleased with his choice of service. They work them terribly hard and the discipline is something, but Harry is an orderly sort of person and does not object to strict discipline.

It would be nice if 'B' would get his orders for he is frantic over all the delays. He was finally called for his physical and mental tests for officers' training and also had an interview with some army officers. He sold us on the idea that they would not take him and then in came a notice that he was accepted. Great rejoicing all round. But so far no orders have arrived and he is living from mail to mail, always thinking that tomorrow he will be called. This weekend he was so discouraged about his status that he wanted to go to the draft board and ask to be drafted. Bill thinks that he should wait but I hope it will not be for much longer. His usual good humor is cracking.

Don became dissatisfied with his education because he did not think it was preparing him for the future, namely for war. Because he is a good student and had taken almost enough subjects to be a graduate now, he was able to go at once to college. He is not far away, only about one hundred and fifty miles. There he is taking huge doses of mathematics and physics. It is tough work but he feels that it is just what he wants to help him get in the navy. In fact, he expects to enlist in about two weeks. If his class work is satisfactory he will probably get his preliminary training this summer and then be allowed to return to his studies until called. Somehow, I hadn't thought that Don would go off so soon and I miss him rather badly but he is very happy and feels that he is doing a man's work. He certainly looks like a man. Since he has lost so much weight you are more conscious of his height. It is a bit dull for Cliff without the boys, but he is used to the old folks and has his own friends and seems content. We are certainly glad to have him to cheer us up and to hear his youthful voice about the house.

Did I tell you that we had put Cliff on a modest allowance from which he has to buy all clothing and pay for all movies etc? So far he has been a miser, but he is threatening to buy a flannel shirt as he is very short of them. When we first put our boys on allowances they didn't buy any clothes so that we had to demand that they look respectable and it looks as if Cliff is not going to like giving up money for clothes. We will tell him if we think he is shabby. He is reaching a dressy stage, so I hardly think we are likely to have to do much urging when spring comes. Last summer's things are much too small. He will tower over you, Grace, when he comes home.

When we were in New York we were startled at its appearance dimmed out. It has always been so gay and bright that it was hard to recognise it somber and black by night. The gasoline shortage is worse in the seaboard states as they only get three gallons per week and we learned what our feet were made for. Fuel oil is also scarce and the houses are decidedly cold as a great many people heat with oil still, in spite of the government's warning that it would be wise

Bill Matthews with his first grandchild, another William (known as Terry in his early years), Glendale, 1943.

to change to coal. Fortunately our house is warmed by good old coal and we merely have to be sure not to be wasteful.

Since so many of the older boys are away, Cliff's age group is being called upon to take on church duties. Last Sunday Cliff was an usher and took up the collection. He and Dave Peck made a fine pair as they marched up with the plates. Bill and I smiled admiringly as he came down the aisle and one of our friends told us that we looked like two doting old hens. Nice people in the village aren't they?

I almost bought a silly hat today but I was with a sensible friend and she looked so horrified that I decided it would be better to put the money into war stamps. Too bad, it was so jazzy, it would have been good for morale.

It is time to sign off now. With a great deal of love from us all.

Jean Strohmenger to Grace and John Mathews

6 February 1943   77 East Main Street, Peru, Indiana

It has been such a long time since I have written that I don't know where to begin. I believe our last letter was written just after Christmas to tell you that we had received the Christmas presents. Since then we received the telegrams, the books, a letter, the broadcast and another letter. We appreciated everything.

Your broadcast came over perfectly. We heard every word and Josie did fine. She'll have to go some to be able to catch up with her sister Sheila, though. Since we have come here the girls have gone through the 'poor little refugee' stage all over again and the folks all act as though they had just arrived from England. At first I thought that I would not let Sheila go out giving all these talks, especially since we were writing up a new one for each occasion, but finally we got one speech written up and she gives that one every time. She has talked to four or five different organisations and more loom ahead for the future. I guess the practice will be good for her. I told her that she would probably have to be making speeches when she got back to England to tell the folks over there about her life in America, so by the time she is thru she should be quite a public speaker. You know, I feel sorry for Josie when your family all get back. She is going to have to take the same back seat that Gloria has had to take here. Grown people can be so cruel sometimes.

The reason I haven't gotten around to writing is that I never seem to get above water in all the things I have to get done. We are on the go all the time and when not on the go I've got so much work to do just to catch up. This past two weeks we have had a run of sickness. Dinah started and we all followed on. Warren has been having coughs and colds off and on ever since we have been here. I think the navy practice of drinking has lowered his resistance. Before we came and he was living with the fellows at the 'Y' they all had a glass before dinner and for any other excuse they could find, so I can say, 'It serves you right', now that he has these colds because he never had them at home.

Warren has been quite busy lately. He had three brain concussions in four days – two of which died. One was a plane crash, the first fatal one since this base was started in July. Then two nights after a sailor skidded in his car and was hit by one coming in the other direction. He lived only a couple of hours. Warren gets all these cases because we are at Peru and all the other doctors are in Kokomo.

The girls all got good report cards. I guess Wyoming is a very good school after all. Sheila and Dinah didn't miss any school with their colds. I think if Dinah wasn't so darned curious she wouldn't have caught this last cold. However, the colored children in her class are such a curiosity to her that she had to get well acquainted with them (to the extent that two little colored boys and one tough little white were under our window singing love songs to her last Saturday). And, too, Dinah's burning desire to see inside a 'trailer' caused her to work up quite a friendship with a little girl who lived in one. A trailer is one of those homes on wheels that the very wealthy and the very poor hitch onto their cars and get around the country in. The wealthy use them to go to California and Florida in the winter and the poor use them for alltime homes – and this isn't Florida.

Dinah still goes on with her fibbing. One day when I was sick Warren gave the girls some lunch money and told them to try the cafeteria across from their school. When they got home I asked them what they had eaten. Gloria said she had pop to drink with her food. Dinah said she had milk. I knew that if Gloria had pop then in all probability Dinah had the same. So I asked her why she said milk when she knew that was a fib, and her answer was she didn't think I would have wanted her to get pop. And her table manners! If Grace needed a stick to get after Cliff, I'm sure she'd better get it out and polish it up for Dinah. (You see, I've been hearing tales out of school about the stick.) Dinah wants to lie on the table. She is too weak to lift her hand to her mouth to feed herself another bite, but lays her arm on the table and turns her head around and down to pick up the bite. She still doesn't chew her food as though there were any reason for her doing it or that she was ever supposed to get through.

You probably think I am a horrible old devil to talk about Dinah like that, when you would give the world and all just to see her. I guess I'm doing it to a certain extent to warn you of what you're in for when she gets home and also to protect myself when they start telling tales out of school about me. You'll have to let me know how you work it out. I must confess that I get nowhere with Dinah. I can reason with Sheila and Gloria and sometimes when they get started with a job they get enthusiastic and really do a good piece of work, but Dinah . . . I realise that it is my fault too. I should be able to cope with her, but I just see red instead. If she were my own I'd give her a good sound licking for some of her tricks, but under the circumstances I don't dare. It isn't so much that I'm afraid of you folks but public opinion in our own community might not be so good if the girls went out and said that I spanked them. All I ask is that when they get back you let Dinah know the very first day that you aren't fooled when she tells you a fib. I know now it was a waste of time when I just ignored all her fibbing, thinking that she was afraid of us when she first came here and that after a while, when we would gain her confidence, all would be well. That was a sad mistake. She just thought that I was dumb enough to believe all she said.

It has started to snow again. No wonder the Germans are ready to retreat from Russia. I'm ready to retreat from this snow myself. The war news is more to our liking these days but it still is a long-drawn process, isn't it?

I'll try to write sooner next time, but I have so much writing to do that I never seem to get through.

John Mathews to Jean and Warren Strohmenger

15 March 1943   Hamilton, Hewarts Lane, Bognor Regis, Sussex

Our lives were saved yesterday by the arrival of a really first class lengthy epistle together with some 100% snapshots. We studied the snapshots so many times and so long because we seemed to see such a difference in all the girls. Sheila and Gloria both seem to have shot up, and Sheila in her trousers looks as tall as her mother.

You certainly have a problem with these girls in their new surroundings and, from your remarks, I imagine it has been a trying time for Gloria, but you can bet it is a nine days wonder and I wouldn't be at all surprised to know that by the time you get this letter just about the last thing anyone in town is thinking about will be two girl evacuees from England.

We have talked and nearly sworn at each other since reading about Dinah but I don't think we have come to any real conclusions. I hate to recommend a good spanking because I feel that it is just possible that her experiences over here, although not too terrifying for a grown-up, were possibly more than enough for a child of her age and that she still retains a fear of something unknown or not understood by her.

As far as our feelings in regard to their manners and what not when they get home, please do not let this affect your dealings with the girls in any way. We shall be so glad to see them that we shall not be looking for their failings. We don't expect them to come home like little angels, we prefer them to have a bit of the devil in them, and if they tell *us* stories about you the only satisfaction we shall get is to have a good laugh, and the more laughs we get the better. Grace and I have been married seventeen years this September so there isn't much we don't know about married life. We have our high words occasionally, we always have since we were fourteen, and we have a good many other failings. So don't worry, the only thing that would be likely to peeve us would be to find that you both hadn't any failings at all. Then we shouldn't understand you and you would find us very difficult to live with. Personally, I am happy to leave Dinah's welfare to you.

Grace went off to London one weekend recently because her sister Pat had flu, and left Jo with me. Of course on the Sunday night at about 1 am we had to have a raid. Grace knows the procedure now for waking me when there is something doing. She shakes me very carefully and croons into my ear in a very sweet voice, 'Wake up John deeear, I think a bomb or two has fallen.' But the landlady!! She is another thing. She nearly pulled me out of bed with her first pull and yelled at the top of her voice, 'Get hup Mr Mathews. It's getting 'ot over 'ead.' I thought the darn world was coming to an end. My heart did about 160 and I didn't know for a moment whether I was coming or going. Old Jo woke up and in a protesting voice said, 'What is it Daddy?' After assuring her it was only practice firing she promptly went to sleep again. The incendiaries looked as if they were falling close to a point which I won't mention, and I had to get to the nearest phone to make sure things were all right up there. I got Grace's bike out but the lamp would not function, so I borrowed Win's, got about a hundred yards down the road and my coat tail caught in the back wheel and over the handle bars I went, luckily on to the grass verge. So, in the end, I decided to do it the hard way and got the car out. After phoning, I found everything was OK, and when I got back Jo was still sleeping soundly, so I then indulged in the inevitable cup of tea by which time the All Clear was going and off to bed I went again. It's a great life if you can stand the pressure.

We have just been listening to a broadcast from the US called 'Answering You'. The NBC apparently set out to answer questions sent in from this country, and it was very interesting. A number of people in Times Square were invited by a bloke with a travelling mike to give their impressions of the English. Apparently there is going to be a very welcome influx of American visitors after the show to see the ruins over here. I hope they'll get a good look at me.

The idea of the navy habit of drinking on every excusable and some inexcusable occasions lowering Warren's resistance to colds is bunk, lady (do I sound American?). A couple of highballs twice a day is as good as ham and eggs to any man feeling the weight of wartime responsibilities. I wish I could afford them, but with whisky at about five dollars a bottle it can't be done except on occasions.

Having heard that coffee was very scarce in America, I wrote off some days ago to find out whether I would be allowed to send you some. That sounds like sending coals to Newcastle doesn't it, but actually we don't have much difficulty in getting it here owing possibly to the fact that we do not drink so much as you people. However, I have had no reply yet, possibly because they consider the request too daft to be worth answering.

Well folks, I had better get this letter off or I shall not get it away this week. Cheerio and keep smiling.

DINA MATHEWS   SHEILA MATHEWS   GLORIA STROHMENGER

Sheila and Dina Mathews, English girls residing with Lt. and Mrs. Warren Strohmenger, 77 East Main street, and the Strohmengers' daughter, Gloria, pictured above, have been doing their bit in the war and have received citations for their efforts, it was revealed Thursday. The children have given their hair for use in instruments of war and for needs of science and industry.

It has also been learned that another Peru youngster, six-year-old Carol Jean Blackmore, daughter of Mr. and Mrs. J. S. Blackmore, has joined in the campaign for blond hair by contributing hers.

The children sent their hair to the Bendix Aviation Corporation after pleas had been sent out by the government for long, straight, blond hair, for use in instruments and other war materials.

Fireman Dies On Locomotive

C. A. Bunnell Stricken Wednesday Evening

Charles A. Bunnell, 50, a Chesapeake and Ohio railroad fireman, died suddenly at 5:30 o'clock Wednesday evening while at work on his switch engine, near the Main street intersection of the railroad. Death was said to have been due to coronary thrombosis.

While Mr. Bunnell's health had

The certificate of thanks received by the girls stated that it was "for the gift of human hair, from which selection will be made for use on instruments serving the nation's war requirements and for the needs of science and industry. By the above kind act not only has the national need been facilitated, but the funds of the USO and Red Cross have benefited as the cash market value of all hair used is being paid into those patriotic and humanitarian societies." The certificate was signed, Julien P. Friez and Sons, Division of Bendix Aviation Service. Hair submitted must be straight, blond, untouched by chemicals, hot irons, waving machines, etc., and at least of 14-inch length and may be sent to the Friez company at Towson, Md., the certificate stated.

Over 8 Million In U. S. Forces

Call 300,000 a Month From Manpower Pool

Washington, May 6.—Manpower Chief Paul V. McNutt indicated today that approximately 8,300,000 men and officers are in the U. S. armed forces now.

McNutt did not use that specific figure in testifying before the house military affairs committee, but he told the committee members they

Dinah, Sheila and Gloria do their bit for the war effort. A report from the *Peru Daily Tribune*, 6 May 1943.

Jean Strohmenger to Grace and John Mathews

19 June 1943
United States Naval Reserve,
Aviation Base, Peru, Indiana

I wish we had enough room to invite Cliff up here for a few days. I know he would be thrilled to death with the base. The girls are getting pretty much used to it by now although they get excited sometimes. Warren is going in to his tenth month here at Peru. He surely won't be here much longer.

Warren won't be home tonight or tomorrow night. He is relief officer tonight and tomorrow he is medical officer of the day. My, did they have a busy day yesterday. It started at 7 am when the cadets took off and ran into heavy fog. Twenty-one out of the 27 Stearmans had to make emergency landings in neighboring fields and when they tried to get the planes away later in the day several turned over or cracked up. Later in the afternoon one of the jeeps turned over and a plane crashed, in both cases resulting in bad injuries. Warren went out with the ambulance and brought the pilot back. The poor boy really got his face messed up and one eye gouged out. Warren was afraid he probably had a basal skull fracture too, but when he talked to me over the phone this evening he said the boy seemed to be coming along all right.

After all that Warren was tied up in the operating room and didn't get home for dinner. We drove out to the base to see the movie *Prelude to War* and picked up Warren from the dispensary to go over to the show. Even then the excitement didn't let up. A big storm arose and the lightning hit the electric wire, so the movie and lights went off for a while. Then they called for one of the classes of cadets to report to the field immediately, what for we didn't know. They stopped the movie again after that to call for Dr Strohmenger and we knew that meant a crash. Then again they stopped the movie to ask all the cadets to report to the field immediately. We learned that they had to have the boys to help hold the planes down that were still on the field. It took five boys for each plane. No one was hurt in the crash so Warren finally came back in. I couldn't tell you a whole lot about the movie, though.

Lt Commander Mattison's wife was asking me the other day if I had heard anything about sending the children back. She said that she had read in her home town paper that they were sending them back now. I haven't heard anything about it, but I think I will write to the Evacuee Committee in New York and see if it is so. Our status is so uncertain that if the children are being sent back it would make it a lot easier for us, especially since apartments are so hard to find these days. There still seems to be bombing over there, but maybe they realise that Germany can't keep it up, so they want to have the children ready to go when the time comes. Now maybe you will all believe me that the war can't last much longer – on the continent at least.

I'll close now and get to my radio news before it is too late. I can't miss any of the news these days. It is too good.

'B' and Janet Matthews in the garden at Trelawny.

Janet Matthews to Grace and John Mathews

27 July 1943 Trelawny, Glendale, Ohio

It certainly would be convenient if I kept a carbon copy of my letters for things happen so fast and furiously here that I cannot remember what I have told you and what priceless gem of information may have been omitted.

The big news is of Harry's marriage. Quite suddenly he was given nine days leave and as it is doubtful when he will be in Glendale again for a long time the children decided that they would like to get married. It was a very pretty wedding, quite simple, but I have never seen the church look lovelier with white gladioli on the altar and tall candles at every other pew tied with big white bows. Betty made a really beautiful bride and Harry looked extremely nice in his sailor suit. We had expected 'B' to be here as his training course happened to end about the same time as Harry's leave began, but his orders didn't come through and so he was not here and Don acted as best man, dressed to kill in a white suit belonging to his father. Cliff was an usher and was so handsome and young that he almost stole the show. He wore a white suit and a dark red tie, looking very serious but with the rebel curl falling down on the forehead every now and then. As all the other ushers were from out of town it was up to Cliff to see that all the close relatives were properly seated. He was so nervous about his responsibilities that he was looking pale when he left for the church, but he did nobly and I think he enjoyed himself very much once he got busy. Harry gave his ushers each a small key ring with a little disk attached with initials on it and I noticed that Cliff's was extra special with a picture of St Christopher, the patron saint of travellers, on it. I mention this merely to show you how the boys feel about Cliff. I was amazed myself because Harry is a heathen as far as church-going is concerned but he evidently thought it was just the thing for Cliff.

Harry can get to New York in a few minutes from his post so Betty and another girl are trying to find a small apartment in the area. Harry will have two days once a month as long as he is stationed there and a few hours now and then. Sounds a little bleak to me but they seem very happy about the arrangement and he will not get so homesick with a wife to hold his hand.

I think I have mentioned that Harry is in the Coast Guard and 'B' in the straight navy. The Coast Guard is a separate service in peacetime but in war it is part of the navy. Even so, they do not seem to have the same arrangements about time off as the navy. They are generous with a few hours but stingy with days. The navy seems to keep them hard at it for several weeks or months and then suddenly gives the boys time to go home. I rather think I told you that 'B' had been promoted to chief petty officer. It is a fine thing to be from a monetary standpoint as your uniforms are issued to you and you do not have to buy them like a commissioned officer, and the pay is about the same as an ensign. 'B' has been sent to Oklahoma and as Cincinnati was on the way he had five days at home. He and Mary left today to drive out there. He thinks that he will be able to spend some time off the base so they hope to set up house-keeping if they can find a place to live. We hear that it is terribly crowded there but they will not be particular about their abode if they can be together. Ain't love grand? He doesn't wear a sailor suit any more, but still looks pretty neat in his coat with the red emblem on the sleeve and his nifty white cap with visor. He doesn't know exactly what his work will be but it will be in the line of training other men. None of the married men were sent immediately to sea which is great for their wives. The day will come, but meanwhile he will have a chance to be with Mary for a short time at least.

Well, enough about our family and over to yours. I am sorry to have to report that Lonsdale is losing ground. Cliff has a new girl named Bea Burchenal and she is a distant cousin of Bill's. She is the best tennis player in the village, in fact, played in a state tournament and didn't do badly. She has mops of hair which is not perfectly straight and a thin little face. The effect is piquant rather than pretty. She is quite slight but can hit that old ball with the huskier ones. I think Cliff must be badly smitten because he spent his hard-earned cash to take her to dinner and a movie last Saturday. It also cost bus fare and he took a terrible razzing from 'B' and Mary about squandering what they referred to as a 'fortune' on a girl. He dressed very meticulously, dark trousers, contrasting coat, red necktie and SHINED shoes. We made him come in and let us admire him and 'B' kept saying, 'You'll knock her dead in that outfit, kid. If she doesn't fall for you tonight, she's crazy.' Cliff looked horribly embarrassed but sort of pleased too. You would think from the way I talk of Cliff's wardrobe that he was Adolphe Menjou.[1] The truth is that he

[1] A dapper American actor, 1890–1963, who played supporting roles in *A Star is Born* and other well-known films of the 1930s and 1940s.

has very few things. The white suit at the wedding was borrowed for the occasion as there wasn't one to be bought in the city of Cincinnati and as Don and one other usher were in borrowed clothes it was quite the fashion.

By the way, don't tell Cliff that I mentioned his new girl. He would be ready to wring my neck. He has been very quiet about the whole thing and had he not taken her on the spree we would not have known about the infatuation. He had to explain why he would not be here for dinner and that is how we got the lowdown.

Clifford Mathews to his parents

4 August 1943   Cottage 82, Harbor Point, Michigan

As you can see by the address, we are no longer in Glendale. Mr and Mrs Matthews and I were invited up here for about three weeks by Mr and Mrs Ralph Rogan, relatives of Mr Matthews. They live in a huge house with terrific grounds in Glendale and their 'cottage' here resembles a hotel. I am the only young person here but I have managed to enjoy myself thoroughly so far.

I have to dress up for meals but aside from that I am very comfortable. We eat at 9.00 am, 1.30 pm and 6.30 pm and the Rogans go to bed at 9.00 pm. Mr and Mrs Matthews and I stay up as long as we can for we can't stand twelve hours sleep every night. It's just too restful!

Harbor Point is a small peninsula, about a mile long, sticking out into Little Traverse Bay. Between the curved peninsula and the mainland is a very good natural harbor. It is very deep, deep enough for lake freighters to enter, and is fed by springs from the floor of the harbor. Consequently the water is very cold and it takes a lot of will power to dive into it. In this harbor the Rogans have their own dock at which they moor their schooner the *Wild Goose*. She really is a beautiful boat, about 46 feet in length and a two-master. She sleeps four and has all the accommodations such as a galley. Yesterday afternoon we went out sailing and I took the helm for about ten miles. Mr Matthews has steered it before and we had a lot of fun seeing who could push it over 7 knots.

Just before we left for the boat a maid handed us a letter from you which made the day perfect. Both your letters are so interesting and I love them because they are from you. Before me I have a letter from Dad that I have read over and over. It's the kind of letter I'o like to get more often for it really helps a boy who worries quite a bit about the future. As soon as we get back to Glendale I am going to look into the matter of those examinations. However, about all I have learnt in the academic line at Glendale High School is that Washington crossed the Delaware, which wouldn't go far in my London matriculation. About my ambitions for a career. I hope you don't mind my saying rather bluntly and I hope it won't hurt your feelings that I have no interest in chemical research but I have just about decided that designing is the thing for me. I agree most emphatically with you when you say that people my age should begin planning and taking courses that will help them in future life. Most of my friends have no ambition, which to me is a great shame. I think that as I am very interested in aviation that field of design would be the most interesting for me. I have to talk all of this over with Mr and Mrs Matthews and see about the examinations. I certainly would like to gain a degree but right now it scares me terrifically. I'll write you soon about it.

Well, I'm fifteen years and four days old. 31 July was a marvellous day and the watch Mr and Mrs Matthews gave me was much too good. It really is a beauty. Mary and 'B' are sending me a razor out from Oklahoma which really makes me feel old. I shave about once every two weeks, by the way.

I'm reading Wendell Wilkie's *One World*. It has sold more copies than any other book in America. Try and get hold of it. It's rather anti-British but I haven't thrown it in the fire yet.

Well, take care of yourselves. If the good news keeps up I'll be seeing you inside of a year.

John Mathews to Jean and Warren Strohmenger

16 August 1943   Hamilton, Hewarts Lane, Bognor Regis, Sussex

It is about twelve days since I posted my last letter to you, and we had just received that morning your letter of 19 June as I mentioned at the time. I had not read yours when I posted mine, so I will deal first with the most important part of yours – the girls coming home. We have not contacted anyone yet who has had a child come back, but I heard of someone yesterday whose girl arrived here safely and I hope to contact her next week to see how it was managed. In

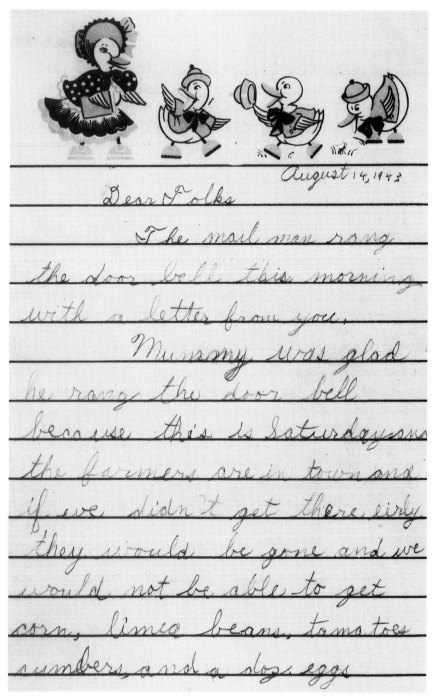

August 14, 1943

Dear Folks

The mail man rang the door bell this morning with a letter from you.

Mummy was glad he rang the door bell because this is Saturday and the farmers are in town and if we didn't get there eirly they would be gone and we would not be able to get corn, limea beans, tomatoes cumbers, and a doz eggs

A letter to Grace and John from Gloria, 14 August 1943.

the meantime I have written to the United States Committee for the Care of European Children in London, who deal with all queries both on this side and on yours. I wrote to Miss Noel K Hunnybun, who has just returned from the States and who actually had been in Cincinnati and had seen Mrs Clark, and had heard of the Mathews kids. I explained the position to her, that you had had to move to Peru owing to Warren having joined the navy, that you felt your present address was far from a permanent one and that if you were stationed elsewhere things would be easier for you if the children came home. She appreciates the position, of course, and is writing to Mrs Clark to see what can be done.

I have told Miss Hunnybun that I do not want the girls to come over by ordinary sea route but that if arrangements could be made for them to fly or come by a neutral vessel, such as a Portuguese ship, as far as Lisbon and then fly from there to England, the risk would be much less and in fact would be practically confined to the flight from Lisbon. Very few planes on that route have been shot down, I believe, although I am not sure of that, of course, because they only report such losses when the plane contains important passengers like Leslie Howard.[1] Miss Hunnybun has suggested that we leave things to her for the time being as she is in possession of information which cannot be divulged concerning routes and before making any arrangements she is writing to Mrs Clark. Strangely enough, Grace has just shown me today's paper in which it stated that twenty-five children had just flown from Lisbon to this country. They had been in America about the same time as the girls, but it did not mention how they got to Lisbon. Two small boys were dressed in pale blue uniforms with 'HMS' on the epaulettes which, they explained, stood for How Military School in Indiana. They were only about eight and ten. Well, well, I wonder what will happen. We are anxiously awaiting your next letter to see what you have learned over there. Miss Hunnybun said that it would be a little while before she could write us again because of the time the mail takes. It doesn't seem quite real that we might be seeing the girls in the comparatively near future, and we are not banking on it until we know the facts. I expect we shall hear that the children that have come over are the offspring of rich families who have paid about £300 for their passage. We'll see.

---

[1] The distinguished British actor, producer and film director who was killed on 1 June 1943 when the passenger aircraft in which he was travelling was shot down by German fighters on a flight from Lisbon to London.

I see from Sheila's letter that she thought my special letter to her in our last but one mail was just exactly right. I'm glad she thought so. She also says that she just hopes it is true that the English children are coming home. Frankly I'm rather surprised. I guess so many people have solemnly assured us that our children would never want to come home after having such a marvellous time that we had begun to believe it ourselves. It's nice to know that they still have a soft spot for the old geezer.

You will have seen by this time that certain spots along our South Coast are taboo to visitors just now. This and a new form of kerosene rationing is making me very busy. I have to be driving nearly all day and dictate my letters over the phone. I have 266 small and large business people to call on and explain the new scheme to, and, believe me, 90% of them would be lost in Dinah's class at school. I can tell by the vacant expression on their faces that they are not taking in the scheme as I try to explain it to them. I'll admit that most of them are already nearly driven crazy with the other rationing schemes they have to contend with. By the time I get home at night I am nearly crazy myself.

I wish you could be here when our planes are going out to bomb Italy. It is really a terrific sight. All along this coast wherever you look there are huge bombers gaining height as they go out over the Channel. There is no secret in this as the papers print it. The noise is almost terrifying and if they were Jerries it really would be. In the news today it states that in the second quarter of 1943 we have dropped 36,700 tons of bombs on Germany compared with 700 tons on us. They dropped 18,900 tons on us in the quarter when the girls left for America, compared with the 2,750 we dropped on them. They certainly started something when they began that game. It looks like another twelve months will see the European portion of the Axis finished, and then for the Japs.

This is Sunday evening, and I have to buzz off in a minute to go on fire watch at the depot five miles away. I never want to work the day after fire watching, somehow. I usually have a thick head from too much smoking and not enough sleep.

Well, I have to get along, so will wish you all the best and love from Grace and Jo.

Clifford Mathews to his parents

7 September 1943   Trelawny, Glendale, Ohio

I'm afraid I have been very lazy about writing to you lately but I have written to Grandma Whittle and Uncle Tom since I wrote to you last and have been keeping up a pretty regular correspondence with Hugh and my sisters.

We've been home from Harbor Point for about two weeks now after having a marvellous vacation. Travel is rather difficult nowadays, although it's probably nothing compared with England, and we couldn't get train reservations all the way home. However we went by train down to Grand Rapids, slept the night there and then drove down by way of Jackson and Lansing in the car, which had been driven up for us the day before. The trip was 324 miles and we did it in about ten hours. It was my first long motor trip and I really enjoyed it. Michigan country is very much like Ohio, rather flat and ordinary, with a little village about every five miles and a fair-sized town every twenty miles. These little villages are nothing in beauty compared to ours in Hampshire, which we used to drive through on Sundays. The typical American village is just plastered with metal advertising placards. I was amazed when I first came over by the variety of signs but I've gotten used to them now.

Before lunch today Mrs Matthews and I listened to Mr Churchill speak from Harvard University. He was made a Doctor of Law and a Historian and made one of the Honorary Alumni of the college. President Roosevelt is a Harvard man himself. I hope you hear Mr Churchill as I thought it was one of his more informal and best speeches. While talking of 'this new era of locomotion' he was referring to the internal combustion engine and instead of saying internal he said 'infernal', at which the gentlemen of Harvard roared and roared. However Mr Churchill refused to chuckle and kept repeating 'internal, internal' as if to remind himself never to say infernal again.[1] I read the other day that Mr Roosevelt is considered to be much more popular in England than he is over here because of the old party problems. I wonder if that's true of Winston Churchill?

Tomorrow I start school but I'm not going back to Glendale. After talking it over with Mr and Mrs Matthews I decided to switch to a bigger high school, which is situated nearly in Cincinnati. The

[1] This 'slip' had in fact been carefully rehearsed.

school is a huge place and offers great chances in the line of scholastics and athletics. A group of us from Glendale are going and I'll tell you more about it when I've been there for a while.

If Jo is enthusiastic about birds as you say in your letter she would love Florida for there are really some beauties there. At Harbor Point there were millions of little martins that used to skim across the water at a terrific rate. They were marvellous to watch. Jo is probably a big girl by now and I'd give anything to see her, and you of course right now. I'm still hoping for a good picture of you both but you're probably very busy.

The news nowadays is really terrific. This Italian campaign is zipping along in marvellous fashion. You know, Montgomery is very popular over here with people my age. He's a great guy.

I'll write you next of my adventures at my new school.

Cablegram from Bill Matthews to John Mathews

14 September 1943

HAVE JUST LEARNED GIRLS SEEKING PASSAGE
HOME COULD THEY JOIN OUR HOUSEHOLD NOW
REDUCED IN NUMBER FOR THE DURATION OR AT
LEAST UNTIL PASSAGE SAFER A CABLE GIVING
YOUR CONSENT WOULD DELIGHT US WE WOULD
THEN WORK ON IMMEDIATE TRANSFER
THROUGH AUTHORITIES HERE

Cablegram from John Mathews to Bill Matthews

September 1943

MANY THANKS FOR YOUR OFFER HAPPY
CONSENT SUGGESTED TRANSFER BUT FEAR
MISUNDERSTANDING HOPE TRANSFER CAN BE
ACCOMPLISHED WITHOUT HURTING
STROHMENGER FEELINGS

Janet Matthews to Grace and John Mathews

15 September 1943   Trelawny, Glendale, Ohio

Last Saturday night after dinner I said to Bill that it was high time that a letter went off to England. He agreed and then took to reading the paper, so you can guess who proceeded to type. In the midst of the letter-writing the telephone rang and it was Sheila asking for Cliff. He had gone out so Sheila and I had a little chat. She told me that she and Dinah had applied for passage to England and asked if Cliff's papers were in order. I was struck dumb as this was the first word we had had on the matter. Sheila said that they had heard that four hundred children were going home.

I asked to speak to the Strohmengers to try to get more information about the plan but they were out and were to leave for Indianapolis at noon the next day with Gloria, leaving your girls here with the grandparents. We tried all day Sunday to get in touch with the Strohmengers and Cliff went down to Wyoming but we could not locate anyone and they got off without our talking to them. Bill then called Mr Alter, who is head of the committee in Cincinnati in charge of English children, and he said that he knew nothing of this plan and that he thought that about ten children had gone back because they had become of military age. During my conversation with Sheila she said that the Strohmengers had been unable to find a large enough apartment in Indianapolis to house them all. Then the case-worker, Mrs Clark, called and said that a letter from England had been received saying that you were not enthusiastic about the girls crossing at this time.

Well, we immediately thought how perfectly wonderful it would be if we could be so lucky as to have the girls come and live with us. We talked it over with Cliff and he seemed thrilled at the prospect and with his help we concocted the cable to tell you of our idea. I then told the authorities that we would like to have the girls and thought it would be nice for the children to be together. But I made it very plain that we did not wish to do anything underhanded, or to try to snatch the children. I left it that we were most anxious to have the girls and hoped that it would be an arrangement that would suit everyone. We have now received your cable and hope that you will feel that we have not done anything tactless. We think that we understand just what you meant to convey, namely that you would like the children to be together, but that you naturally feel that every effort should be made by the local authorities and by us not to hurt the Strohmengers' feelings. We will try awfully hard to live up to your request. You see, the trouble is that we have gotten so fond of the One Ts that the thought of having those irresistible children is fearfully exciting and it is hard to sit by and let some old committee decide the matter, but it will be good for the character. I hope the matter will soon be decided as we are in a dither over it.

No doubt Cliff has told you about his change of school. When we came home from Michigan we found that a number of parents had decided to send their children to school in town. At first we rather hesitated to send Cliff because we dislike the daily trip. But, after thinking it over, we decided that it would be an interesting experience for the boy to attend a large American public school. This particular school, Walnut Hills, is considered to be the best in the city. Cliff rides in with Dave, Jim Whitney and Ted Poor in a car driven by a schoolteacher. She lets them out about a half mile from the school and they walk the rest of the way. They get finished at three o'clock and ride back in a private car three days a week and the other two days can walk half a mile to a bus which brings them right to Glendale, taking about half an hour.

Don is taking his exams this week and that will end his freshman year. He comes home next Monday to enlist in the navy. I cannot believe that this war has reached out to my youngest son. I still think of him as something of a baby in spite of his six feet. He has maintained honor grades throughout the year and it is too bad that his education must be interrupted but he is young and maybe he will pick up where he left off.

Harry has just been told that a move is in the offing. Just what it will be he does not know. He rather hoped that he would be given a chance to improve his rank, but he is not at all aggressive and 'B' says that you must push a bit to get ahead. Funny thing, 'B's pep is one of his attractive characteristics and Harry's shyness is his most beguiling trait.

Terry[1] remains with us as 'B' and Mary are still in one room and the infantile paralysis epidemic continues to rage in Oklahoma. He is now ten months old. He is big and husky and the girls would love him (now don't get back to that subject, Janet!). Still no teeth but you can see he is not going to have little pearls of teeth but great big whoppers.

---

[1] William Procter Matthews, born 11 November 1942.

The news from Italy seems better tonight. We have had the situation in Salerno[1] terribly on our minds these last few days. I think we were foolishly happy over the surrender of the Italians, not stopping to think of what a bloody battle it would take to get the country away from the Germans.

Well, I must send this off. We promise to behave as you would wish us to, for we do not want to have you think less well of us.

Jean Strohmenger to Grace and John Mathews

20 September 1943   1211 North Alabama, Indianapolis, Indiana

Well, the orders that I had been anticipating came fast and furious. On 7 September, one year to the day since Warren reported at the station, he got his orders to go to Indianapolis, Indiana, to be Senior Medical Officer in charge of Induction at the Federal Building and Armory. I had started the girls off to Peru schools that very morning. Warren had to be here in Indianapolis on the 13th to start his work, so we took the little three-room furnished apartment that the doctor whom Warren was replacing left. There was nothing to do but take Sheila and Dinah back to Wyoming and get Grandma to look out for them. I tried to make it plain to the girls that they would have to look out for themselves for the most part and keep their room and bathroom in order because Grandma is past seventy and can't be running around doing for them the way I did. This was the best arrangement we could make and I felt that possibly in a month or so permission would be coming through for them to start back for England.

Gloria and I had to stay in Peru until we could get the furniture started back to Cincinnati and the few things we were bringing here loaded on the navy bus for Indianapolis. Indianapolis is only about fifty miles from Peru, so we don't feel that we have gone anywhere at all and I might add that Warren is fit to be tied. When he went to take his physical to go into the navy, he came home and said that he surely hoped that he didn't get induction work as that would drive him nuts – so here we are.

---

[1] Scene of the main Allied landing in southern Italy on 9 September 1943. The Germans resisted fiercely and for a time threatened to drive the British and American forces into the sea.

When we got here on Saturday we found a letter from Mrs Clark wanting to see us right away in Cincinnati, or else she would come here. We had just been down to Cincinnati when we took the girls there, so we asked her to come here. I hope Mrs Clark will get here tomorrow if she is coming. I am anxious to hear what she has to say.

I don't know whether Sheila and Dinah will do so well about writing letters now without me to get behind them and make them. We got two from them last week but I think it was just to let us know how they were getting on. Grandma won't be the type to get after them. When I called long distance last Friday night to tell the folks that the movers were coming for our furniture the next day I asked what the girls were doing and learned that Sheila had skipped off to Dottie Sloan's for Friday night and was to be gone for the weekend, although Sheila had promised me that she would clean up upstairs on Saturday. Maybe it will be good for all of them. Sheila and Dinah are prone to sit back and let somebody else do all the worrying, but when things get bad enough they will have to do their own worrying.

I think we are going to get a rest here in Indianapolis. There is no navy life here. We are going to join a couple of clubs, but there won't be the social life that there was in Peru for me. We all hated to leave Peru. We had had such a good time out at the station and also at the country club. The townspeople went out of their way to be very nice to us. The girls hated to leave the schools, although Sheila and Dinah were glad to get back to Wyoming. We can't understand why the navy couldn't have given Warren the same post in Cincinnati and saved us all this high rent and extra expense. Things never work out that way for us, though.

Everyone is ready to go out for a walk, so we'll get these letters in the mail. I have written quite a few today.

Cablegram from Bill Matthews to John Mathews

28 September 1943

TRANSFER ACCOMPLISHED DECISION MADE BY
AUTHORITIES BELIEVE NO HURT FEELINGS
CHILDREN ALL SEND LOVE

John Mathews to Jean and Warren Strohmenger

28 September 1943

Hamilton, Hewarts Lane, Bognor Regis,
Sussex

We had a cable today from Mr Matthews telling us that the girls had been transferred to them. Not knowing all the facts, I can only imagine what has happened. We had a cable a week ago telling us that Mr and Mrs M had heard that the girls were arranging their passage and asking our consent to transfer the girls to them rather than risk the journey by sea at this stage. I replied to the effect that we consented on the understanding that there was no mis-understanding and that it was all being arranged with your approval. What I thought had probably happened was that the girls knew that you were enquiring about the possibility of them getting a passage and had in their excitement overstated the case when talking or writing to Cliff. He in turn thought the thing was almost fixed up and the Matthews immediately sent off the cable to us without making further enquiries. I phoned the Evacuation Committee in London to see if they knew anything of it and the reply was in the negative, but they assured me that nothing would be arranged without them knowing of it. However, as I say, the cable today states that the authorities had arranged the transfer and that there were no hurt feelings. I sincerely hope that that is the case and that you parted with them quite happy that you were doing what you felt was best.

Knowing what I do from the magazines of the difficulty of obtain-ing accommodation at some of the towns in America, I can quite imagine if Warren is to be transferred again to another post you would have had a bad time trying to find rooms, apart from the terrific expense you have had to incur for a place big enough for five, whereas without the girls you would be more likely to get something suitable. We've had the feeling for some time that it was a bit tough on you after you moved to Peru, but we also thought that in your place we should feel that, having had the girls for so long, we would either want to keep them or send them home and not to another family. If that is how you felt, we are entirely in sympathy with you. However much easier it will make things for you now that they have gone, I feel sure that you must have all had a few pangs at the parting and we are terribly sorry that it had to be. One thing we want you to always remember is that we shall never forget your kindness, and that if we can repay you in any way at any time as long as we live we are yours to command – and that isn't just an empty phrase, we mean it with as much sincerity as we can convey.

I cannot write of little things tonight, my brain is working in a groove and all I can think of is the changeover. Grace dreams of the girls at night and I dream about them during the day when I should be thinking of other things. I will write again as soon as I hear more about it from you. I want to get this off by air right away.

In the meantime we send our best love to you all.

Janet Matthews to Grace and John Mathews

29 September 1943   Trelawny, Glendale, Ohio

You cannot imagine how excited we are at having the girls here. It was good of you to send the cable and I hope that you really are happy about the situation. May I just be very frank about the whole thing and then never mention it again? I think that I told you that the children were living in Wyoming with the Strohmenger grandparents while Dr and Mrs Strohmenger and Gloria had moved to Indianapolis, which is a hundred miles away. The grandparents seemed to be very deaf and the children were on the third floor by themselves. In case of illness or fire it seemed to us that it was not a very safe arrangement. Also it was a little forlorn, so we were delighted when the authorities agreed that they should come to us. We did plead pretty hard to have them come to us, so it wasn't quite as we promised, but if you could see how glad they are to be together again you would forgive us. I talked to Mrs Strohmenger for one solid hour on the phone on Sunday and she said that she didn't mind the girls coming to us. I don't think it was easy for them to make such a decision. They had become much attached to the girls and hated to part with them, I am sure. I am urging the girls to write to them often so that they will not feel that we have torn the children away. I also said that at any time that they were in Wyoming I hoped that they would invite the girls to come down and that we would arrange to have them do so.

We decided that it would be good for Sheila to be separated from Dinah some of the time and play with girls of her own age. I hope that you will think we are right. She is such a conscientious little thing that she was always thinking of Dinah. So we have sent Sheila

133

to a school for girls in town. She leaves on a school bus at eight and gets home at five in the afternoon. It is what we call a country day school and I am sending you a brochure about it. The girls have their sports at school as well as music and the regular lessons. Sheila seems very enthusiastic about it. There are a great many Glendale girls going there and they have a gay time on the bus. The school require that the girls wear a uniform. It is a green jumper, pleated from neck to the hem and tied with a belt so that even the most slender child looks like a sack of meal. It is certainly not glamorous but they tell us is an exact copy of an English girl's hockey costume. If that is so, I am all for it. I will say that Sheila looks darling in it.

Dinah goes to the Glendale public school. She seems to like it very much. There are a number of very cute little girls in her grade and she has brought someone home every afternoon. She does not seem at all lonely and is pleased to see Sheila but is often so involved with her own pals that she just says 'Hello'. Tomorrow, Dinah is going over to join the young choir. They wear red vestments and I can hardly wait to see her. I shall probably burst with pride when I see her walking up the aisle even if the only claim I have on her is that she pronounces her last name the same as we pronounce ours. Grace, you cannot imagine how strange it is to see girls' dresses in this house. I shall never forget those blue coats the girls wore when they came to this country. I can see them still the way they looked the first time I saw them, blue coats and hats and string gloves. I hope I shall have as good taste when I select any clothes.

Please don't think we have forgotten our first love, Cliff. He is as fine as ever and so proud of the girls. He is delighted about the school that Sheila is attending as most of the girls he knows go there. It is called Hillsdale, by the way. Several of the girls who like Cliff and several of Don's flames are being especially attentive to Sheila. Each child has something to tell of the day at school and dinner is full of innocent amusement. We love it.

Don is home, having finished his freshman year with high honors, I cannot resist adding. He is keen about your whole family and you would have smiled to see him out with a flashlight this evening looking for Dinah's homework which she had mislaid in the yard. I think you would like Don, he is nice. There have been times when I think he has been just a little jealous of all the fuss made over Cliff but he has never said so and they have been extremely congenial of late.

Don tried to enlist in the navy today, but they will not take him

Grace Mathews – and Clifford's old bear – at Hamilton.

until the twenty-fifth of October. He was pretty sunk about it because he wants to be up and at it. So we are going to send him to see Harry and Betty for a few days. Once the boys are in the service it will be hard for them to get together. Don has only been in New York once or twice as a baby and I think it would be a lark for him to see the big city. It is hard for him to wait around as there is no one his age about and he finds us comfortable but boring. You know the age.

Terry has a tooth, got it just yesterday. At present it barely shows. In fact, I have to keep tapping it with a spoon to convince Bill and Don that it is still there. He is simply thrilled with the girls. They push him about in his little scooter and he looks at me as much as to say, 'I used to like you, but this is the life.' Mary and 'B' are still trying to find a place to live so that they can have the baby. Of course, they have no idea how long they will be at the camp. 'B' might be transferred elsewhere or sent to sea.

This is a terribly short letter but I did want to get off a note to thank you for entrusting the girls to me. We will try hard to be worthy of your confidence. Anyway, we haven't had a letter from you in so long that you don't deserve anything longer than this. I hardly dare to joke with you for fear that you will come back and say that you have been too overworked to write or ill or something. If you have some good alibi just forget the whole thing.

PS
Two gallons of gas a week now for us and two pairs of shoes a year. This is certainly going to be difficult with Cliff. His feet grow about an inch a month.

John Mathews to Janet and Bill Matthews

5 November 1943   Hamilton, Hewarts Lane, Bognor Regis, Sussex

We have just received two letters, one from you and one from Sheila, both of which we had been looking forward to with a great deal of anticipation and curiosity to know just what had happened and what the girls thought about not coming home. Now we have had the letters we are completely happy about the whole thing. You seem delighted to have them and the girls are certainly delighted to be with you. Sheila says in her letter, 'We are the luckiest girls in the whole world' and certainly I know a lot of girls who would agree with her. Her letter was the longest and most interesting we have yet received from her, and one could tell that she was really bubbling with excitement and thrilled with everything.

We had a letter from Mrs Strohmenger today which, before we opened it, we thought would give us her views on the matter but no, it was written the day before she saw Mrs Clark. We had received a copy of the declaration we had to sign to receive clearance for the girls' passage, which included such phrases as 'understand that neither His Majesty's Government nor any other person ... will be responsible for fatal injury or damage to the children during the journey.'

We really do understand the Strohmengers' position in all this. The fact that they did not want them to go to anyone else goes to show that they had become attached to the girls. They have done a great deal for the girls and we shall never forget that. Even so, we

925 Congress Ave.
Glendale, Ohio
Weds. Oct 27, 1943.

Anything I loves' a huddle

Dear Mummy Daddy and Josie,

I quite excited because next weekend
we are going see Hugh. He is the first member
of our family we've seen in three years. But
I won't be able to see him much because
I'm in quaraentine for scarlet fever. Yesterday
I was just about to give my oral preport for
Eivics when the headmistress came in and told
us a girl in our class had it so the whole
ninth grade have to stay in their rooms till
next Tuesday. I am in our room and Dwial
is in Don's room. He went to New York
to visit Harry and Betty. He will get back
Friday and then Saturday when Hugh comes

One of Sheila's letters to her parents, 27 October 1943.

137

had the impression from Mrs Strohmenger's letters that the girls were becoming rather too much for her and that a change was indicated, even to the extent of risking a passage home, if that was the only way out.

We now know that over 300 children did obtain passage in a Portuguese ship to Lisbon, but they came without any guarantee from the British authorities that they would be given air passage from Lisbon home, with the result that most of them are still stranded there. They appear to be the children of wealthy people as I see several of the parents are titled, and no doubt they paid the heavy dues for the passage. Sheila and Dinah would probably have had to come back in an ordinary ship in convoy. Very fortunately for us you stepped into the breach and solved our problems completely.

I only hope you really are getting as much pleasure out of having the girls as you try to make us believe in your letters. Quietly, of course, we are green with envy. We imagine you all sitting down to supper with the youngsters telling of their day's experiences and a good deal of laughter going on just as we used to have at Rushington Lane, our last home.

Looking again at the last batch of snaps you sent us, one shows a pretty nice spot of motor car in the background. Being a male I would cast my eye on that. I'll bet it rides like a dream. My old tub has its advantages – any time you are feeling a bit liverish a short ride will shake up your innards nicely. I'm running around just now with a cracked cylinder head and I'm likely to have to suffer with it for some time too because new heads are like lemons over here, pretty scarce.

I'm supposed to have it greased and serviced once a fortnight but labour at garages is so scarce that one has to go down on one's knees to get a job done nowadays. However, I mustn't grumble as I am lucky to be running a car. Cliff remembers in peacetime the lines of traffic that sometimes used to build up on our weekend runs. Now you hardly see a car on a Sunday, and very few during the week.

Well, I do not want to overwork the censor, so I will close for the time being with tons of love to you all from the family here.

John Mathews to Jean and Warren Strohmenger

Hamilton, Hewarts Lane, Bognor Regis,

20 November 1943   Sussex

We got your letter yesterday in which you blew off steam a little regarding the methods adopted to take over the girls. You can imagine how difficult it was for us to visualise the situation. All we knew at the time was that Mr Matthews's cable gave us the impression that the girls would be sailing at any moment, and that they would be delighted if we would consent to them going to the Matthews household for at least a few months. It would have been a very difficult thing to do to cable back and say, 'Nothing doing', so I did the next best thing, as I thought, and cabled that the transfer should go ahead only on the understanding that you were quite happy about it, and my letter to the Committee in London was to the same effect. We cannot give orders to the Committee of course, and their decision while the girls are in America is final as far as we are concerned. We thought that everything had been arranged eventually to your satisfaction because the next cable said, 'Transfer arranged. No hurt feelings.' This apparently was not the case. I am very sorry indeed that the thing was not done with your complete assent, and that the old people were put out. It was very good of them to undertake the job of looking after the girls.

I really would like to meet some of those friends of yours who jumped to the conclusion that it was those English so-and-so's who were to blame for what happened, just to find out on what they base their ideas that an Englishman is just naturally sub-human. I'd like to bet that most of them have never been over here, and probably have never even spoken to an Englishman. I don't say the attitude of mind is peculiar to Americans – there are plenty of Englishmen who think the same of Americans – but whether it is one or the other I get just as mad. The war is helping a lot to eliminate the silly misunderstandings which exist on both sides. As I write the Warning has gone and I have just been outside where I could see the flash of bombs being dropped in the distance and a red glow in the sky.

Your friends can say or do what they like but we shall always remember your kindness to the girls. Actually we hate being under an obligation to anyone, but at the time the girls went overseas things were so bad that we just swallowed our pride for their sakes.

Tell Gloria we hope she is not missing the girls too much and that they will all get together whenever you get back to Wyoming. Mrs Matthews has promised to arrange that and we should very much like to know that they were keeping up their friendship. I had given up all hope of finding anything to send over for Xmas, but went into a jewellers in Chichester and asked if they had anything which could be sent over without your having to pay a high import duty. To my surprise they told me that if I could find any articles of silver which were over a hundred years old I could probably obtain a licence to export them, and there is, they assure me, no import duty over on your side. Then began the hunt and I eventually discovered some 1812 salt cellars, bought them and set about getting permission to export. I am still trying. Believe me, getting anything of this sort out of England is much worse than getting blood out of a stone. The post office couldn't tell me how to do it but advised me to write to the Board of Trade, Liverpool. The latter advised me to write to London. London were so long replying that when Grace went up I told her to take some more forms to the BoT and stay there until she got some action. She got her brother-in-law to do it. He was told it was absolutely impossible to export antiques in precious metals. By this time I had received a licence and phoned to tell him so, at which he was amazed. I was then instructed to apply to my bank for a form CD3, fill it in and return it to the bank together with a letter to the Bank of England asking their permission to export without repayment. I have done this and am awaiting their reply. I am told the latest day for posting is next Wednesday, so I am beginning to lose hope of getting them to you before the bells ring out. Anyhow, you will know that I have done my best. The strange thing is that they apparently belonged to someone with the initial S, so you will be able to say they are an heirloom.

I wish we could send Gloria something, but tell her that the sort of toys that are being sold in the shops over here are such rubbish that she wouldn't look at them twice. There has been quite a scandal about the price charged for such things as a toy engine made from odd bits of wood, cotton reels and an empty 'Vim' container. Not that Gloria would want toy engines, but everything else is on a par with that example.

Drop us a line and let us know how things are going. A Merry Christmas to you all and love from the family.

Janet Matthews to Grace and John Mathews

27 November 1943   Trelawny, Glendale, Ohio

The other day when I went to the mailbox, I found two letters from England and thought, 'Hot dog, we've hit the jackpot.' But, one was for Harry and one for Don. Well, you know how the old curiosity works, and I thought of opening them very skillfully just to learn what was cooking in England but my Mommy taught me that it was not cricket to open anyone else's mail so they were forwarded unopened. It was really swell of you to write to the boys and they will be thrilled. A letter from England is a major event and when you are in the service mail is the breath of life. Thank you so much for taking the time and the trouble. Two days later we were rewarded by a lovely letter of our own.

To continue with the question box department – Dinah's friend Emily is Emily Richardson. There is an enormous tribe of Richardsons in Glendale. They are all nice. Emily looks like a little brownie. She has a small round face with rosy cheeks, stiff little pigtails with ribbons on the end. She is full of pep and talks incessantly. We took Dinah and Emily into Cincinnati to a movie on Friday evening. They were like two little squirrels, they flew around every which way. They got in a revolving door and made it spin so fast that no one else could get in. They went down the street with arms about each other not looking where they were going and bumping into people, they were so busy both talking at once. Bill and Sheila and I laughed until we were weak. Bill called them gremlins and that was not a bad name for those two merry little people. It occurs to me that this may sound like a complaint. It is decidedly not meant as such but just to give you an idea what Emily is like and the amount of energy generated when Dinah and Emily get together.

You may also wonder where the ambassador was (I think of everything). I cannot remember exactly what Cliff was doing that evening but he was probably at a movie in Wyoming with the boys. He has reached an age when a little family party is not his idea of a good time and THAT IS ALL RIGHT. We understand and he knows that he is always welcome on any of our little sprees, but would usually prefer the company of his contemporaries. As a matter of fact he is sweet with the girls and the baby and his old folks.

The teacher at school tells me that Sheila is very popular and they always say to me that she is making a fine contribution to the life of the school. I can believe both statements. We think she is darling. We thought that Sheila looked a bit pale and thin when she came. But she really looks lots better now. I think she is as happy as she could be away from home. Her appetite is wonderful and I think she must be getting more sleep in a bed to herself. Anyway, the added weight has taken the pinched look from her face and we think that she is lovely. The truth of the matter is that the girls are spoiling us and you are going to have to unspoil us. I came home from the city yesterday all tired and dirty and up popped Sheila with a cold glass of Coca-Cola. I almost fell dead. The boys would all gladly get you anything if you asked for it but they never think of having it ready for you. Bill and I had to get all dressed up the other evening and Dinah told us with such enthusiasm that we looked nice that we went off feeling like the Duke and Duchess of Windsor. We aren't used to being pampered like this and it is going to ruin us.

We had some pictures of the children taken as a Christmas present for you. I think the one of Dinah is not quite as satisfactory as the others. It really doesn't do justice to her, but it will give you an idea of her size and the whole cute little figure. I am anxious to hear what Grace thinks of the girls' dresses. They were my first venture into the realm of girls' attire. I am afraid I have gone in rather heavily for ruffles over the shoulder but it seems to me that both look well in that sort of thing. I do hope you think so too, Grace, though I realise you are too tactful to say that you don't agree.

One of the effects of war in this country seems to be that courtesy has been lost to a large extent. I suppose it is the result of taut nerves. When I asked for directions in a store recently the saleswoman said to me, 'There's the sign, can't you read?' You have a moment's irritation and then you think that perhaps she has a son or two on the high seas or in Italy. I am going to try to cultivate an extra share of tolerance and courtesy.

Cliff is learning to drive a car. Whenever Bill is driving in this vicinity he gives Cliff a lesson. He has made a bargain that he will do this provided that Cliff will help Sheila with her dancing. Dinah is too young to be included but is so busy with her own affairs that she hardly notices when the other two are away.

I must sign off now and go to church. We all send our love and wish you a merry Christmas.

Extracts from Clifford Mathews's diary

8 December 1943   Trelawny, Glendale, Ohio

I sent off such an awful letter to you on Monday that I decided to try to make my letters more interesting by setting them out as a diary of daily events. I'll try it for a week and then send it off to you. Let me know whether you like the idea.

Wednesday 8 December 1943

Dinah woke me about 7 am and it was pitch dark so I'm sure if it hadn't been for her I would have overslept. Good girl! Rode to school as usual with Ted and Dave, with Mrs McLaren at the wheel. Boy, she's an awful driver. She never changes gear all the 12 miles (slight exaggeration). Swimming practice after school. After one false start I did the 40 yards in 21.7, my best time. Today was last practice before the meet tomorrow.

Got three rides home and arrived here about 6 o'clock and to make the day perfect there on the desk was a letter from you – and addressed to me. I have gotten quite jealous of Mr Matthews as it seems all the letters have been addressed to him. Inside the envelope were two letters from you both and a super picture of Mummy. It really is appreciated and it's sitting on the desk in front of me now. Mummy doesn't look a bit older for the three years and just as beautiful as ever. Now a photo of the handsome moustached guv'nor to put on the other side of the lamp and all would be perfect.

Thursday 9 December 1943

Today was the day of our first swimming meet, held at Withrow High School here in Cincinnati. It was exclusively for novices who had not been in the teams of their respective schools in previous years. Withrow has an enrolment of between three and four thousand pupils and is really a huge place. We started off by winning the 120 yard medley relay (breaststroke, backstroke and freestyle, each boy doing two lengths – 40 yards). I swam the freestyle. We won just about everything but I was worn out by the relay and came in seventh with a time of 23.4 seconds; very bad! Our straight relay team went wild and finished about 20 seconds before the next team. Of course, we were all very jovial and on departing threw the usual wisecracks at the losing team, making ourselves thoroughly repulsive.

Friday 10 December 1943

My new issue of *Flying*, to which I subscribe, came today and in it was an article by Peter Masefield[1] in which he goes off the deep end raving about the P-51 Mustang as the world's most perfect aircraft. I don't think it can be so perfect for one hardly ever hears of them being used in combat except for shooting up trains. Of course, I have pretty firm opinions when it comes to that sort of thing and I think Mr and Mrs Matthews must be sick of hearing about the Royal Air Force and the Fleet Air Arm. They left for Chicago to see Don tonight.

Saturday 11 December 1943

Tried playing the piano with Sheila in the morning and listened over the short wave radio trying to get the BBC, but all I could get was 'les bombardiers des Américains et Anglaises ...' In the afternoon we played some basketball over at the town hall. Basketball is my least favorite American sport but one gets plenty of exercise.

Thursday 16 December 1943

We really whitewashed the guys at Withrow. The seniors won by 34 to 22 and we trounced the juniors 34 to 5. We came close to breaking the record for the straight relay.

Janet Matthews to Grace and John Mathews

26 December 1943   Trelawny, Glendale, Ohio

This year is the first time we have ever had a doll under our Christmas tree! There was also a kitten and Bill is being very amusing about it. He claims to dislike cats and will not take the slightest interest in it. For some reason it is being called Murphy, and Bill's only comment is that we will probably find that it should have been called

---

[1] Now Sir Peter Masefield, Chairman, Brooklands Museum Trust. On active service as a war correspondent with the RAF and US Army Eighth Air Force, 1939–1943. Chairman, British Airports Authority, 1965–1971. Chairman, Board of Trustees, Imperial War Museum, 1977–1978. Masefield was right about the P-51 Mustang, which proved to be one of the outstanding aircraft of the war.

Mrs Murphy. I must say Murphy has been no trouble to anyone so far. Sheila warms its milk, adds a bit of bread and a nibble of meat and it seems to thrive.

There was quite a crowd for dinner and in the kitchen a sixty-year-old cook with high blood pressure, so we all pitched in. Dinah and I decorated the table. Sheila helped with the cooking and a very fine meal came of it. Everyone kept leaping from the table to serve someone else and most of the time there wasn't anyone sitting down, but we had a good laugh. It was three in the afternoon before we had the dishes washed and everything put away, but the cook was still alive and we had enjoyed ourselves. We took a brief nap and then started to help 'B' and Mary get ready to leave in the morning. We were up at six-thirty this morning to see them on board the train. It was frightfully crowded and there were two other babies in the same car. I should stay away from railroad stations these days. They make me feel like crying. The soldiers and sailors look so young and so many of them have babies with them and I get thinking of the broken homes all over the world and probably I get feeling sorry for Janet Matthews and the first thing I know I am fighting off a good attack of the weeps. The hardest thing is this everlasting saying goodbye to your boys in the services. Don will be home in two days for his 'boot leave' and then off he will go again.

A most amazing and exciting thing happened yesterday. We had a communication from Buckingham Palace, with greetings from the Queen. I have had fun lording it over Cliff, for he hasn't had any personal messages from the royal family.

Later Your cable came the day before Dinah's birthday, and was she excited. Nine years old! It happened that the Russian ballet was here and we went in to see it. We were very fortunate as the program was a colorful and lively one. Cliff couldn't bring himself to go (our boys have refused to be taken to ballet) but Bill went along and spent most of his time watching Dinah. She sat on the edge of her chair with her eyes open as wide as they could go.

It is high time to sign off. We send all sorts of affection to the One Ts. I rather tremble when I think of 1944 and what it may bring, but maybe it will be a happy new year.

Extracts from Clifford Mathews's diary

Tuesday 28 December 1943

 It started to snow this morning about 10 am and it came down so thick that by 1 pm Sheila, Dinah and I were able to don our coats and galoshes and throw a few snowballs at one another. This evening after dinner, Dave and Tom came over and we went down to Gunny Hill with our sleds and did a little coasting. There weren't many people on the track and we froze in the driving wind but it was fun to come home to some hot Ovaltine anyway. There must be almost six inches on the ground. Don arrived on furlough.

Wednesday 29 December 1943

Everything is coated with a thick blanket of snow and it's really beautiful. This morning all the young people decorated the Lyceum for the dance this evening. We put up so much green stuff it looks like a forest and smells like one too! We coasted on Gunny Hill this afternoon. The track was a little faster but still not up to par. I read in this morning's paper that the *Enterprise* was in this latest action with the German destroyers. Grand piece of work wasn't it? I must write to Uncle Harry.[1]

Thursday 30 December 1943

It was a very good party last night. It was Sheila's first dance and a great success for her. She looked very pretty in her new white evening dress and got her card filled for all the dances. I was so glad, for I was as scared as she was as to how she would go over with the boys. Mr and Mrs Matthews came at about 1 am and brought us home in the car for the snow is rather deep.

Friday 31 December 1943

The dance last night was given by the ATC and BTD sororities. Sheila, of course, being a BTD, went and took a date. In sorority dances,

---

[1] Engineer-Commander Henry Leonard Mathews RNR, who was awarded the DSC for his part in an action in the Bay of Biscay on 28 December 1943 when the light cruisers HMS *Glasgow* and HMS *Enterprise* engaged a flotilla of eleven German destroyers, sinking three and damaging others.

when the girls give the dance, they are entitled to ask the boys. It's kind of tough on the boys, but the girls have fun for once. Mr and Mrs Matthews came to get Sheila early because they didn't think it wise to let her stay to the end, having been out the night before. It was a fairly good dance but one of the Glendale boys got dead drunk and sort of spoiled our evening. To see a boy, only fifteen years old and one of your best friends, so drunk that he is actually unconscious, is rather startling.

John Mathews to Sheila and Dinah Mathews

12 January 1944   Hamilton, Hewarts Lane, Bognor Regis, Sussex

Thank you for your lovely letters. They cheer us up tremendously. It is just about time for another one so every time the post arrives we look to see if there is an American stamp.

Your photographs arrived safely and we think they are absolutely super, in fact the nicest possible present. You both look simply spiffing. Both of you seem to have put on weight and look as fit as fiddles. What wouldn't we both give to be able to give you a hug and a kiss. I suppose we shall have to wait a little longer for that. I hope it won't be so long that you will be too shy to kiss us when we do see you. Sheila, darling, you look such a grown-up young lady in the photograph that my depot clerk thought you must be about seventeen instead of nearly fourteen. Next time you write tell us how tall you both are. You remind me of the words in *Red Riding Hood* where the wolf says, 'And what lovely eyes you have, my dear'.

By the way, I tease Jo when I am reading *Red Riding Hood* to her by saying Red Rooding Hide, and she gets most annoyed. She still jumps into bed with me very early in the morning and insists on my continuing with a serial story, of which we have an instalment every day. I have to make them up as I go along and we are now in the middle of one about two Scotch terriers, one of which is all black and the other all white. I wonder where I got that idea from? They have smuggled themselves away on a big steamer. The instalment always ends just as Mummy comes in from the bathroom. I usually try to end on a terrific climax, for instance this morning the captain was looking all over the ship for them and was just about to find them when the instalment ended. You should hear Jo give a tremendous sigh when I say, 'And I'll tell you tomorrow just what happened.' When I came home this evening, she said, 'Daddy, if you'll tell me what happened to Mr Chips and Daisy (the names of the dogs) I'll promise to forget by tomorrow morning.'

Mummy would be writing this to you but she is frantically finishing snappy scarves for saucy sailors. She has promised to write a long one next week without fail.

Aunt Janet and Uncle Bill send us good reports about you but I've a sneaking feeling they wouldn't tell us if you were naughty. However, I expect you are not *too* bad. Some boys and girls are very prone to take everything for granted no matter what is done for them, and they seldom think of saying 'Thank you' as if they meant it. There again, I'm *sure* you are not like that!

Did Mummy tell you how thrilled we were to get your lovely Xmas card on Christmas Eve? It came just at the right time and the wording inside was really the most complimentary thing we have ever had said of us. We felt that we really did still mean something in your young lives. It is still in a place of honour over the fireplace.

So you had a delicious dinner at Grandma Matthews. Your description made our mouths water. I hope she was as pleased to have you as you were to be there. Talking of dinner, I noticed that American soldiers over here all cut their food and then change the fork over to the right hand and eat with the fork only, leaving the knife on the plate. Does everyone do that in America? My district manager says no, so I want inside information.

When you see Mr and Mrs Carruthers again, please thank them for us for having you over to dinner. You do get around don't you? We shall feel a pair of old stick-in-the-muds compared to you. The things you do in one day would have made a good week's fun over here for you. Does Dinah still sing in the church choir or has she been turned out for giggling?

We think it a great idea that you girls have found your own friends and are not dependent on one another as you might have been in Indianapolis.

You (Sheila and Cliff) should get along much quicker with your languages now that you can quiz each other in the evenings. I'm awfully glad to know that you do so. I wish you were both here – I would start learning Latin myself, maybe.

So, you only take a puff at a black cigar every once in a while. Oh well, that's different. We thought you might be smoking a box a week. You're better than we thought you were obviously. What does Dinah smoke, a pipe?

148

Well, we are very glad to know that you are all so happy. Who wouldn't be happy with Aunt Janet and Uncle Bill?

Cheerio, sweethearts. Tons of love and kisses from Jo and Mummy.

Janet Matthews to Grace and John Mathews

8 February 1944   Trelawny, Glendale, Ohio

You should see the room in which this letter is being written. Betty is sitting on the floor writing a letter, Harry is bending over a table making a design for a toy box. Dinah is also on the floor cutting out some pictures for a scrapbook she is making for the children's hospital. Sheila is reading the latest letter from 'B' and laughing over it. Cliff is sprawling in a chair drinking a bottle of Coke and joking with Harry. Who says that we are not the luckiest people in the world?

It is beginning to look as if we might go to Florida. While Bill has been well for some time, the doctor wants him to have some rest. Bill and I would go on ahead to get things sorted out and the girls would follow with Jane Ann our maid. Walnut Hills are very snarky about letting people off school, so Cliff would have to travel later, alone one way, and that thrills him. We hate the idea of going off without him but I am anxious for Bill to get the rest.

Grace, my dear, I feel terribly about your idea that I am without fault. Of course, I lie to you in letters so you will think I am faultless, but I shall hasten to show you that I am a bad-tempered old woman. In the first place, I am FAT. I am extremely untidy and also a born nag. I goad Bill and the children until they could cheerfully murder me. I used to get so mad about 'B's behavior that I would spend a whole meal telling him off and many is the time that I have hit my own children – not yours though. I am selfish and extravagant and cannot keep my accounts straight. Bill is truly a saint to have put up with me all these years, anyone in the village would tell you that. My face is what is called expressive, which means it is a mass of wrinkles. You would look so lovely and young to your small fry. When I see the beautiful knitting and hear about the sewing you do I cringe with inferiority. I want you to be happy about the children and not think of them living with a cross between a glamour girl and a paragon. I shall not bother to refute John's statement that he is a freak. I would tell him what we think but I have your word for it, Grace, that he doesn't need building up.

I am haunted by the thought of the boys on the beachheads in Italy. Things do not seem to be going well. We went to church on Sunday *en masse* and I watched the people coming down from the communion rail and thought of each one, 'He has a son in Italy, her daughter is in India with the Red Cross, here is the mother of three flyers, the father of a missing son.' It seemed almost unbearably sad even in this tiny community and then I multiplied it by the world and it seemed impossible that so dreadful a thing could have happened to us. I hope those that clamor for peace now will some day see the light and realise that we must go through with it this time and settle the world so that there may never be such a time again, or at least a fair chance that countries may live at peace with one another.

Bill thinks I should mention that now that the children are all under one roof they often have a wonderful time talking of home and things they used to do, and the nice people in England. They are very very proud of you all and were annoyed that John said that Josie was not pretty. We all agree that she looks very pretty.

The idea of no mail for a while is repulsive to us. John, you will have to try to write whether it is on a lorry or in your sleep. If it means that the invasion is on, I guess we will have to put up with it.

A great deal of love from us all.

PS

So glad to hear that Grace has that little weakness for crazy hats. I bought one this winter with a feather pointing out over my nose. It scares me so that I have only had the nerve to wear it once or twice.

Extracts from Clifford Mathews's diary

22 February 1944

Today was the anniversary of Washington's birthday. All the city schools were given a vacation. I woke up in the middle of the night to find my curtain being whipped high in the air, rain pouring in through the window and a regular gale blowing outside. I lay awake for a long while listening to the wind howl. I still have that same false feeling of security with the blankets drawn up around me and the storm without as I did as far back as I can remember. It rained just about all day then cleared up, as it so often does, in the evening and the sunset was beautiful. I walked down to the village for some notebook paper. When I got back I remarked on how nice it was outside walking and Sheila and Mr and Mrs Matthews decided to take a stroll and they are still out.

Friday 3 March 1944

I got home so late from the meet last night that I was too tired to write. We had a very successful evening at the YMCA. Both our teams, junior and senior, won the city championship. We, on the junior team, won with quite a few points to spare but the senior contest was very exciting and we won by only two points. Everybody was plenty happy and after we tossed our managers in the pool with all their clothes on we began tossing one another in and ended in a good old 'free for all'.

Tuesday 7 March 1944

Happy days. A letter from England. One for all of us. Thanks a lot Mummy. I was sorry to hear you had a little relapse but hope you are completely fit by now. Daddy's predicament concerning clothes is apparently somewhat similar to mine, although there is not much *you* can do about it. I'm supposed to buy my own clothes from my allowance but I don't. It's not through lack of funds but my hatred of going to stores and shopping. Mrs Matthews tells me that before they will let me in the cottage at Clearwater I must have bought at least a few things.

Wednesday 8 March 1944

This afternoon we went down to Cincinnati to see Tommy Dorsey and his orchestra on the stage at the Albee. Featured was Gene Krupa[1] (Don's idol) on the drums. You may have read that Krupa was recently in jail for selling narcotics to minors or some such deed. The show was really good.

[1] A celebrated drummer of the swing era, who later led a successful band of his own.

John Mathews to Janet and Bill Matthews

8 April 1944   Hamilton, Hewarts Lane, Bognor Regis, Sussex

Well, as I write this I presume that you will be basking in the Florida sunshine, drinking fruit juice (I hope) and I expect Cliff is sailing to distant parts of the globe – in his imagination – in the *Totton*. We sincerely hope that you are really enjoying the holiday and that Bill will feel rested and fit for the battle again on your return. I forgot to mention ices, and I suppose that is because they just don't come into one's mind over here now. I suppose it must be at least two years since I tasted a real ice. It's certainly going to be a great treat to see a sundae once again. I expect my lunch yesterday would make you look rather askance too. I had it at a café next to the Odeon cinema in Bognor. It consisted of one slice of pork, three half potatoes and about a tablespoon full of cabbage, followed by a small portion of boiled rice with half a dozen raisins in it, and a cup of tea. Still it suits me as I don't really like a heavy lunch, otherwise in my old age I am sleepy in the afternoon. You don't have cafés *in* cinemas as we do over here, I believe.

It can be very useful if one arrives in the middle of a film, as is usually the case with us. I can never get Grace to the cinema before the beginning of the feature film. As a matter of fact I am having a day off today, Easter Saturday, and I have, I believe, broken the spell because lunch is being served at this moment – 12.45 pm – which should leave us time to get there by 2 pm. I am afraid Jo is very young for films but she has to go along and she tells me that she likes plenty of shooting, because she knows they are not real bullets but only smoke!

. . .

We are back from the flicks, and I regret to say that we did not break the record, we actually arrived about five minutes after Bob and Bing started on *The Road to Zanzibar*. However the film made up for it by being very funny. We like their humour. Do you?

We had a letter from Sheila and yourselves just after I had posted my last murky effort. Sheila was very very excited about the prospective trip to Florida and terribly excited also about the outfit which you bought her in the city. She seemed to think that the lady waiting on you was very ambitious because she got not only three blouses, but also four playsuits and summer dresses. It's my guess that the lady who was doing the buying didn't need much persuading. Of course, we are green with envy. Those girls are living in a sort of fairyland. I wonder what their thoughts are sometimes and whether they pinch themselves to see if it is only a dream after all. I'm sure Sheila and Cliff appreciate all you are doing for them and I'm hoping that Dinah is not proving too impossible. I told Cliff to smack her if she needed it, but I thought after I had posted the letter that I might be getting him in wrong with you if he took my advice. I must restrain myself in my advisory capacity and leave it to someone who is obviously better able to cope with children than I ever was.

Jo has just asked me whether you would be having Easter eggs but I couldn't tell her because I don't know whether you indulge in chocolate Easter eggs in the States. We always had them before the war but I think they have ceased making them since about 1941. She has written a letter to you which I really must send this time because she signed it all by herself. She is afraid the rest of it is a little bit difficult to read, but she has just stood by me and rattled off the whole letter quite as if she could read each word, even to apologising for a mistake and going back over the sentence again, the funny kid.

You were saying that we might be shocked by some of Cliff's attitudes to life and his apparent idea that he knows all. Quite honestly, we hadn't noticed a thing about which we might worry. Not that we imagine he is perfect but just that we realise what boys of that age are like. I know when I was between fifteen and twenty I was terribly dogmatic and argumentative. If I remember rightly, it was almost an impossibility to prove that I was wrong. Grace thinks I'm still like that, which is a ghastly libel of course. Anyhow, I'm quite prepared to hear that Cliff inherited the characteristic and sincerely hope he will outgrow it more quickly than I did.

I'm sorry that you have been put to more expense with Sheila. Strange that both she and Cliff should have one groggy eye. That and the gland which apparently is not functioning properly would probably have gone unnoticed over here at this time. Doctors only call if it is urgent and they are all rushed off their feet owing to the fact that so many have been inducted into the forces. Many many thanks for the way in which you care for our offspring.

Grace has just had a blue fit and her eyes nearly popped out of her head. We get a constant roar of fighter planes here and one of them has been hovering around for a few minutes with a groggy engine. I switched on the radio unknown to Grace, and when it came on with a roar she thought the plane was crashing into the house.

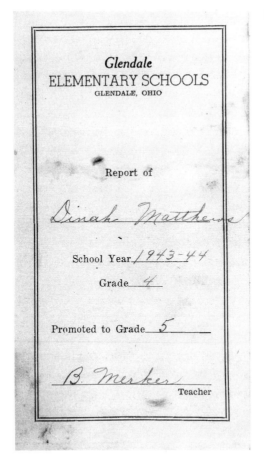

Dinah's school report, 1944.

Glendale
ELEMENTARY SCHOOLS
GLENDALE, OHIO

Report of

Dinah Matthews

School Year *1943-44*

Grade *4*

Promoted to Grade *5*

B. Merker
Teacher

In today's paper it says that weddings between Americans and English girls were taking place yesterday at a London registry office at the rate of one every 15 minutes. If they go on like that all over the country, with Canadians, Australians and New Zealanders doing the same thing, we shan't have any girls left for our own boys after the war.

Well, so long my American cousins, and best love to you all.

Janet Matthews to Grace and John Mathews

7 June 1944   New York City

Your wandering American cousins are in the big city for a fleeting glance at their son Harry. We stepped off the train yesterday morning all unconscious of the fact that the greatest day in the history of the

world had dawned. As we walked through the terminal we heard the loudspeaker announce that it was D-Day. From that moment on we moved in a trance.

All newspapers were sold out but we rushed to Harry's apartment where we hung on the radio most of the day. In the afternoon we went to a cathedral to join the throngs in prayer. It was our first experience of church in New York. In the course of the day we heard the voices of many of our leaders – none more moving than that of the King of England. It was interesting to note the reaction of New York – stores closed, offices closed, radios blared from every building and taxi cab and the churches were jammed. Maybe under its hard exterior New York has a soul.

In a way I am glad that we could be with Harry at this time. He is the one of our boys who is most devoted to his home, most dependent upon us. Nothing in the war has made him feel so keenly that he would like to be doing something more active. He said he felt futile and empty working in this country when events of such importance were going on abroad. We were able to point out that, unglamorous as his job may be, it is of the utmost importance that the munitions of war go out in a steady stream and that it was thanks to thousands of dull grinding hours of watchfulness on the part of the Coast Guard that the stream flowed so smoothly. He thought two days ago that he was to be given the tests which would determine whether or not he could get a transfer, but the examining officer never turned up. No doubt the impending events made it impossible.

Harry tells me he read that there will be no more civilian mail from England for a while. That will be terrible for us, but if we hear nothing we will understand and send our little two bits of news – you will be wanting all the news you can get about the children, I know.

We left your family 'in the pink' of good health, with Cliff in charge for we felt his judgment was most to be relied on of anyone's in the household.

The great news about Sheila is that she has been elected president of her class. It really is an honor as the class officers make up the Student Council and they have a great deal to do with running the school. As a rule, only a girl who has attended the school for several years is elected to this office. Also since last writing Sheila has had a meeting of her sorority at the house. It was in the nature of a picnic and they invited boys. Sheila had Dave Peck as her 'date'. They played baseball, croquet and tennis, and they swam. I think Sheila's enjoyment of the day was somewhat impaired by the fact that she was hostess, but she has carried it off well and everyone had a good time. I was impressed by the good manners of the children – they all came and spoke to Bill and me although we kept very much in the background and let Sheila run the show.

Dinah has been so good that I am afraid that she will sprout wings. I believe Cliff thinks that I am not severe enough with Dinah, but I am stricter than he knows. I don't care much for 'telling off' a child in front of another, so when I have any correction to make I do it between Dinah and me. Now and then we have a little talk and straighten out any problems, but it is usually about small things like tidying her room.

The day before we left Cliff had a DB meeting at the house. *Forty-two* boys came. They are nice boys, or maybe I just like boys – all boys. They had a very orderly meeting, had their annual picture taken and swam and swam. It was like old times to have so many boys about.

John Mathews to Janet and Bill Matthews

11 June 1944 Hamilton, Hewarts Lane, Bognor Regis, Sussex

Have snatched a couple of hours off this evening to write the promised letter, invasion or no invasion. Well, dear people, it has come at last, and when I said in my last letter that it would probably be under way before the letter got to you, I was right. And what an unexpected start it has been in many ways. I quite thought Jerry would have used a reserve of aircraft to try to bomb our airfields and transport and docks to blazes, instead of which we have had only one warning since the start of D-Day and then no raid.

We have seen some sights and the one which will always remain outstanding in my memory was that of Halifax and Lancaster bombers towing glider after glider in one long stream just over our housetop. They stretched as far as the eye could see towards both horizons, troop and freight carriers, and it was a marvellous sight. They passed about 8 pm so they must have landed in broad daylight, and I was hoping and praying that they would get down safely. We read in the papers the following morning that seven of the gliders failed to arrive. It is an awful thing to be looking up at these machines as they go over and know that in all probability some of them will shortly be shot down and the men killed. There was a strong wind blowing and one of them broke a tow rope soon after getting over the sea. The men all baled out safely into the water and were rescued, and the pilot of the glider brought it back to land. I saw it take off the following morning with the men once more aboard.

The weather is our great worry at the moment. It has been bad since the very start except that the wind has only occasionally reached a dangerous velocity. The great snag is that we are suffering from a thick and very low cloud bank which makes it impossible for our bombers to blast the Hun reserves massing in the rear of their beach defences. It was so low on Thursday that even the fighters were unable to do anything for fifteen hours. Apart from that period, though, the sky is always full of planes of all sorts going out and returning. The fighters stay out there if they are covering the beaches for about two hours, then come back and off they go again about an hour later. The only moan they have is that they don't get half a chance at the Hun. If they do get into a scrap they come back full of excitement and begging everyone concerned to get them off again as quickly as possible in order to have another crack.

We are right on the edge of an airfield and the roar of planes goes on all day long when the weather permits and their losses have been *very* light. Of course, everybody was tremendously excited when the day of the invasion dawned and this lasted until the beachhead was established. Now one gets the impression that excitement has gone and is replaced by a desire to get cracking and make this the last nail in the Hun's coffin.

Grace and Jo are still in Wales and Grace's last letter told me that her mother is gradually sinking. It is going to be a little tough on Grace and her sister if Grandma passes away because I can't see any of the male members of the family getting up there just now.

Couldn't finish this yesterday, so am having another crack tonight with one eye open. I received a long letter from Cliff today and he tells me of the terrific expense that you are going to in sending the girls to camp. He does say that Sheila, he thinks, really appreciates what you are doing for them. I sincerely hope so. I have just been looking it up on the map and it looks as though the rail journey alone will cost a small fortune. Why, oh why, is not at least one of your sons working on a job not far from here where I come into contact with US Navy personnel, then he could have made this his home from home.

It is dusk and two or three squadrons of Spitfires are just coming in to land with their lights on after their last run of the day. The night fighters will have taken over. The clouds are still lowering and visibility at 200 feet is just about nil, so send up a silent prayer will you for fine weather. Both your boys and ours want all the air cover they can get.

So long for now and much love to you all.

Extracts from Clifford Mathews's diary

Tuesday 18 July 1944   Trelawny, Glendale, Ohio

 Two more bundles of newspapers from you today, Daddy. Super. I probably will be up all night reading them. I have been doing some reading in *Capital* by Karl Marx. His ideas are very interesting although it is terribly stiff reading.

Friday 21 July 1944

It's now 9.40 pm and the 5th Session of the National Democratic Convention of 1944 has just been adjourned after having nominated Senator Truman of Missouri as the candidate for Vice President. Boy, what an experience. Listening to these conventions has been an education in itself. Uncle Bill explained many of the tricks of the politicians while the thing was going on. I wouldn't have missed it for anything, even though I have been short of sleep in the last two days.

Saturday 22 July 1944

This afternoon Uncle Bill and I played Aunt Janet and Mrs Peck two sets of tennis. We won both sets – Uncle Bill is a good player but I am terrible. A letter arrived from Mummy today. It was the only one that had been opened by the censor in the last half-dozen and it was heavily cut. I completely missed something that concerned Aunty Pat and an apparent robot bomb explosion. Tell me again in the next letter and it may not be censored.

Sunday 23 July 1944

We went out to see Dinah this afternoon in camp. She still seems to be very happy. We haven't heard from Sheila for quite a while – a sure sign that she is not homesick. I have been studying for my History mid-year exam this evening, which will be on Tuesday.

Saturday 29 July 1944

Dave is spending the night with me. We went into town this evening to see a movie, *Two Girls and a Sailor*. It was darn good. I see in the English papers you send that Frank Sinatra is making a hit over there. I thought English girls had more sense. Here one has only to mention his name and the weaker sex fall in a dead faint (on the nearest chair).

Monday 31 July 1944

Today I am sixteen years old. I don't know whether I am terribly happy about it or not. At least I am glad because it means I am that much closer to you. The cable was swell – thanks a million. It came on the right day and I also got a telegram from Aunt Janet and Uncle Bill. I really had a swell day and everyone has been wonderful. It has been the first birthday that I have celebrated in a hot school and the first that I have celebrated by studying three hours in the evening.

I will close my diary here. Take good care of yourselves.

Sheila Mathews to her parents

28 September 1944   Trelawny, Glendale, Ohio

I got all my homework done in school today so I have my evening free and am able to write a nice long letter to you. I took my first typing lesson today and soon I will be able to dash off an interesting letter that you will be able to read.

School is very hard this year. Everyone says the 10th Grade is the hardest of all grades and I am a firm believer in it. We have Caesar in Latin this year and that is my hardest subject. I'm really going to have to work to get any grade at all. English is pretty hard too. We have to read a book a week but that isn't too bad because I love to

Dinah (on the right) at summer camp near Glendale. *Cincinnati Times–Star, 5 August 1944.*

read. We are reading about the French Revolution and that period in England. We are going to read *A Tale of Two Cities* which is really a marvellous book and if you haven't read it you should, it's by Dickens. I love geometry but you really have to keep on your toes in that class. The other subject, French, is quite easy because we are going over some of the stuff I have already had.

I am going to have a girl in my class out for the night. All the girls have people to their house for the night. The girl's name is Helen Martin and she really is a wonderful girl. I was over at her house for a night and her mother and father are very nice and she has two little sisters. The only trouble is that some people don't like her because she is a Jewess and that really makes me mad. Any girl that thinks about creed, color or social position when she picks her friends does not rate very high with me. If the girl is nice, clean and honest I shouldn't think it would matter but to some girls it does.

I am going to go to Cotillion this year but I hardly know any boys except from Glendale and those aren't very nice and Cliff is in Senior Cotillion now.

Isn't the news wonderful? It really is hard to believe. I do hope you don't have any more of those buzz bombs.

We are having a terrific time over here with the election and everything. Most of the girls, in fact all of them, are Republicans and I'm always getting into heated arguments.

Well, it's getting pretty late and I have school tomorrow.

Lots of love and kisses and I do hope you had a happy birthday, Mummy.

Noel K Hunnybun to Grace and John Mathews

London Branch, United States Committee
for the Care of European Children,
Gwydir Chambers, 104 High Holborn,
London WC1

12 October 1944

I hope you are hearing satisfactory news of the children and that they are happy with Mr and Mrs Matthews. I shall be so interested to hear.

In view of the improved war situation, I am now writing round to all the parents who have children in America to ask if they would like to sign the release forms, so that when the times comes for return there need be no unnecessary delays. The signing of the forms merely means that the children's names are entered in New York on the Consul General's list in readiness for return after hostilities are over. I am therefore enclosing two release forms in the hope that you will complete them and return them to me. They should be witnessed in accordance with the instructions given in the footnote.

John Mathews to Clifford Mathews

29 October 1944   Hamilton, Hewarts Lane, Bognor Regis, Sussex

Mummy has been terrifically busy recently and has had to see to moving our furniture from Michelmersh to Totton ... She spent an hour or two in Southampton while she was that way trying to get some wearable shoes and she tells me it would give anyone the willies to have to spend much time there in the state it is now in. The people seem drab and their clothes are worn. There has been no rebuilding yet, of course, and it will be some time after the war ends before the town is in shape again. They have some marvellous post-war plans for the place however and so we must look forward to the day when those plans come to fruition. You are all going to need some courage to keep a smile on your faces when you get back. Totton didn't seem a bad sort of place to you when you were living there, but it is going to seem a little drab when you return to it. I hope to be able to move out of it before many years are past and get something in a more salubrious neighbourhood, although the Rushington Estate is quite good. I think I would like to live in Southampton; it would give you all so much more to do in your spare time with the sports centre, the swimming pool, the skating and music, not forgetting the Dell. Food too will give you a knock because I understand rationing will have to continue for some time after the war. However, I'm sure you will be so delighted to see me again that the details of living will seem a mere bagatelle to you. What a joke!

All this comes from the fact that confidentially I am in a pure funk as to whether you will all settle down again here; however my fears are probably groundless. In any case we shall do all we can to prevent any one of you from getting too fed up with things until you can form new friendships and of course we shall understand if you occasionally get the blues. One thing about it is that you all know something of what has been happening here, and as long as you count on finding us much more ancient in appearance than when you left and the furniture very much knocked about by our tenants and on the probability of having to do quite a bit of bussing instead of motoring, you won't get too much of a shock. Can't tell you how much I look forward to seeing you, old chap, and I sincerely hope that Hugh will come through this business safely so that you will have at least one contact as soon as you get here. I don't know where he is now as I believe he has sailed on a carrier for the East.

By the way, because you don't slip into the habit of smoking and drinking, don't be too tough on the lads that are foolish enough to do so. We are all sinners in one way or another in this peculiar world and we have to be tremendously broad-minded. I know at your age how difficult it is to be tolerant of something which you consider inexcusable but you will find as most people do that as you grow older so you will become less critical and more broad-minded.

Janet Matthews to Grace and John Mathews

27 December 1944   Trelawny, Glendale, Ohio

Remember me? I'm the little woman who used to write to you both with some semblance of regularity once upon a time. Well, Christmas came along and I simply went off the gold standard for a while. Not only was it difficult to get to the city but everything this year had to be packaged up and sent to the boys all round the United States.

The children had such nice presents for us including a lovely bell to use at the table with a fine tone. Sheila had ordered some little cactus plants because I am fond of the funny things but McSnoyd[1] got hold of them and demolished several. He would probably eat raw artichokes if they were available.

Sheila went to a dance last night with Dave Peck. Dave sent her a corsage to wear and she looked lovely. He is definitely her favorite boy. He thinks of her as a mere child I gather, but an attractive one. Pat Carruthers calls her on the phone at least once a day, but she considers *him* a mere child, I'm afraid. That's life for you.

For the first time we are experiencing what is an old story for you. We are worrying about all the boys we have known for so many years. Up till now most of them were in training but those days are over and they are in Leyte, India and Europe. It is hard not to think of all the battles in very personal terms. When there is an advance or retreat in Belgium I hold my breath for fear something will happen to the Burton twins who used to lounge about our living room with Harry and listen to Victrola records. When I hear the Italian news I fear for their younger brother who is there. Leyte means that 'B's closest friend is in the thick of it with the marines. A submarine is sunk. Is young Hugh Garvin on it? Soon it will be our own. It makes

[1] Dinah's terrier puppy.   163

you very solemn and not the best company. I wish we didn't know so many boys so well. Dinah is a fine antidote for this frame of mind with her hundreds of questions as to what kind of tombstone you like best, smooth or shiney, how high can an airplane climb and why? It is impossible to grow morbid when your mind is struggling with those sorts of questions.

I must tell you of one of Dinah's escapades. The Friday evening before Christmas she and Peggy, Emily and Nancy decided that they wanted to go out and sing some carols. It was a bitterly cold night, so I had Dinah put on some long underwear. She thought a dress would be a nuisance, so she then put on her snow suit. With mittens and a scarf and hood she looked ready for anything. But it seems that everywhere they went to sing, they were invited in for a bite to eat. Well, poor old Dinah got hot and decided she would take off her outer wrappings and at several houses sat about munching cookies in just her long underwear. It made a great hit. The end of the story is that I didn't know they had been eating all evening, so when they came in we went out in the kitchen and fixed hot chocolate and cookies and the little monkeys ate as if they had never seen food. No wonder her tummy bulges a bit.

Noel K Hunnybun to John Mathews

United States Committee for the Care of
European Children,
Gwydir Chambers, 104 High Holborn,
21 March 1945   London WC1

Your letter has just come and I hasten to reply at once. I will answer your questions as they arise in your letter.

With regard to the return of the children. I am afraid we cannot make any arrangements for girls to come back on naval boats. I quite agree that this has been done on one or two occasions but how we do not know. We have a definite ruling to the effect that this method of return is only available for boys who have not yet reached their seventeenth birthday. If Clifford returned to England before 31 July of this year it might be that we could get him a 'Special Sailing' by naval boat, which would cost you just a few pounds, as the navy only charge messing fees, but we should have to be very quick in making our arrangements. If you would like Clifford to return by this route, will you let me have a letter signed by you and your wife to say you are anxious for him to return by 'Special Sailing' and that you are prepared to defray expenses up to the sum of £10.

Now with regard to the return passages for the two girls. At present the rates vary between £28 and £35 per person and we see no hope of any reduction. We have made efforts in this direction but have not been successful. I am sorry but there it is. The demand for passages is very great and the matter rests with the respective shipping companies. The parents of children who went out under the care of this Committee only paid about £25 for each child, but at that time the shipping companies gave special terms for evacuees.

I quite agree that most of the children who have returned to this country find their education somewhat behind their contemporaries over here and several of them have had to have some tuition in order to get places in schools on this side. The curriculum is so different in America and many of the subjects which our children start at an early age, such as French, Latin and Mathematics, are often not taken until much later in America.

If there is any chance of my seeing you at any time I should be delighted to do so. I am sorry I have not been able to meet you and your wife, but somehow I have not been in the Bognor Regis district. Maybe later on I shall be able to come down and, if so, I shall look you up. I should give you advance notice of my coming of course.

I hope you and your wife are well and that you are hearing regularly from your children. It is interesting that you thought I was an American. I am thoroughly British!

John Mathews to Jean and Warren Strohmenger

26 March 1945   Hamilton, Hewarts Lane, Bognor Regis, Sussex

I hope you received our cable at Xmas to let you know that we were thinking of you.

Do you mean to tell me you have not received a letter from us since you sent your photograph? I replied almost immediately on receiving it and enclosed some snaps. Your photo is now reposing with our American ones to be framed and hung after the war. It is impossible to get things like that done now. We were comparing it with one or two of the snaps we received when Sheila and Dinah first went to you and noticing how Gloria has changed into a young woman almost from a tiny girl as she was then.

Thank you very much for the Xmas card which arrived at the best possible moment when we were feeling very fed up with life. Just in time to prevent us taking an overdose, in came a batch of mail and cables from America a day or two before Christmas. I had been spending my annual holiday working hard on the house and garden at Totton to put it into a fit condition for reletting, our previous tenants having decided that Xmas was a good time to get out. Grace's sister Pat decided she would like to spend the last ten days of my holiday with us and brought her six-year-old son Bruce and new-born baby Celia with her. This meant I was constantly ducking under rows of diapers strung across the kitchen. Then the baby was taken ill. We had to register for everything like coal, groceries, milk and take out temporary ration cards. I almost had to go down on my knees to get enough coal to keep one fire going. Boy, oh boy, what a life. But now it is March and the sun is shining and they are actually making ice cream again. It has only a small milk content and you have to be around at the right time to get it, but, after nearly five years without, anything tastes good. The cost of living is supposed to be only 32% higher than in 1939 but that applies only to necessities not luxuries such as ice cream and cigarettes, which were eleven pence and are now two shillings and four pence for twenty.

You may have come to the conclusion by this time that we are a little fed up with restrictions and war in general. Well, we shall not exactly be sorry to hear the peace bells ring out. The snag is that although I think the Germans will probably pack up about September, the Japs are likely to prove a more formidable problem than most people think in this country. I hope when we are able to release men from the European front that our generals – I mean those of the United Nations – will decide to make a direct attack on the Japanese homeland instead of trying to oust them from all the conquered countries which they now hold. Once we command the sea and air round the main islands the rest of their fronts will crumble quickly. I sincerely hope so for your sakes, especially as you say that Warren is likely to be close to the fighting fronts.[1]

---

[1] Even as John Mathews wrote this letter Warren Strohmenger was treating the wounded in the front line at Iwo Jima, one the most bitterly-fought battles of the Pacific War.

We are really beginning to wonder when we shall have the children back home again. Maybe by the end of the summer. Housing is such a problem here now that when they do come I shall have the greatest difficulty in housing them unless I can find alternative accommodation for our tenant. The children really are going to get a shock when they get back because things won't be easing up for a very long time as far as supplies are concerned, and life will be tough for a while yet. I've no doubt they can take it but it will be a solemn change for them after Glendale and Wyoming.

We have not seen a V1 for months now and the V2s have not been within miles of us, so we are fortunate in that way. Grace's sister Pat is back at her home in London and says in a letter we received today that she is ready to scream at the slightest thing, her nerves are so badly unsettled. The V2s are about 45 feet long and give no warning of approach. The V1 could be heard a few seconds before it passed or landed and did give time for a dive under a table or into a shelter.

They have cleared the beach near here of mines and entanglements now so we are looking forward to going there this summer. Maybe I'll teach Jo to swim. She is six and a half now and getting tall. She doesn't remember her brother and sisters of course, and displays very little interest in them. I expect she will be a bit jealous when they first arrive.

Well, it's time for bed now, but I'll write again soon especially if I get one from you.

Extracts from Clifford Mathews's diary

Tuesday 8 May 1945, VE Day

At last the real VE Day is here. The excitement that I had expected would accompany this day has been suppressed probably by the fact that a large number of people in this area have boys in the Pacific and also because there have been a great many false alarms. I talked about my returning home with Aunt Janet and Uncle Bill this evening. Aunt Janet said that she would call Mrs Clark tomorrow and see what progress, if any, had been made.

Wednesday 9 May 1945

Goering was captured yesterday. I certainly would like to know where old Schickelgruber is, wouldn't you? They seem to feel pretty sure that he perished in Berlin, *but* they aren't positive. I really believe we must have an edge on Burma by now.

Thursday 10 May 1945

A letter from both of you – happy days. Dinah has received the comics you sent her and I must get her to write you a letter. I agree with you when you say that Dinah will be the 'American' of the three of us. However, she is still young – she will easily change – and you would be surprised how much she still remembers. A little while ago we were talking of our summers at Shoreham and Dinah said, 'Remember the day that I ate half the sandwiches for lunch and the thermos flask full of coffee when no one was looking?' Sheila and I couldn't remember but the 'heftiest' of the three could tell us just what we were all wearing. She seems to remember the holidays much better than any other time.

Thursday 24 May 1945

I talked again with Uncle Bill and Aunt Janet about going home. There seems to be a fair chance that I might be able to come back on a navy ship and they, and I, think this would be the best deal of all.

Friday 25 May 1945

I was very shocked to read of Granny's passing[1] – we all feel very sad about it. I had so hoped to see her again when I returned. Aunt Janet and Uncle Bill are leaving tomorrow for a weekend 'get together' with Don in Chicago. Uncle Bill sent off a cable to you this evening asking your approval concerning return on an RN ship. I have to leave before my seventeenth birthday so there is not much time.

[1] Ada Emily Whittle, died 11 May 1945.

John Mathews to Janet and Bill Matthews

12 May 1945   Hamilton, Hewarts Lane, Bognor Regis, Sussex

Well, it looks as though the Hun has had it at last. Yesterday I spent some time on a large aerodrome on which Lancaster bombers were landing one after the other all day long fully loaded with returned POWs. There were at least four to five bombers circling the drome all the time waiting to land. As soon as a plane got into position on the parking line the bomb bay doors would open and out would fall the prisoners' kit, and the men jumped out of the door and some of them patted the ground and were obviously pleased to be back again. I spoke to some of them and remarked on their fitness, and I learned that this was as a result of the Red Cross parcels they had received in prison plus a wonderful feed-up they had been given by the American troops who had liberated their particular prison. They were full of praise about the way your boys had treated them. It seemed strange that the very bombers which we used to see going over at night with their navigation lights all going out one by one as they went over the coast towards Germany to carry out an operation were now carrying food over there and bringing back happy men. Some of the sayings written on the fuselage in chalk by the men before they left Germany were very funny but most of them rather unprintable. The pilots and crews must have been dog tired, but the happiness of the men was contagious and the crews seemed to forget they were tired and shot off again down the runway as soon as they had discharged their human cargo. Most of them had German badges, caps and so on and I almost asked for a badge, but I guessed they would all have lots of friends they would want to have them.

We hear stories and see photographs and newsreels of people really letting themselves go, but I believe from what I hear happened in the smaller towns the mob instinct was not so prevalent there owing to the fact that the crowds were much smaller. One man in Bognor High Street did throw his bowler hat on the ground and kick it for six and in the evening there was music and dancing in the streets, but everybody was more or less orderly and I only saw two drunks all evening and they were a couple of young sailors, more acting than drunk. I think what kept everybody more or less calm was the fact that all the pubs ran out of beer before closing time and there were no wines or spirits available quite early on.

We had a big bonfire built up near the beach and took Jo along to see it. When we got there it was well and truly under way and to our dismay shortly after sunset, which was at about 9.45 pm Double British Summer Time, the announcer stated that the Fire Service would now put the fire out to conform with the dim-out regulations. These were still in force owing to the fact that a lot of U-boats were still causing trouble. This regulation has since been lifted, by the way, and we are at last after all this time able to leave our curtains undrawn or not as we wish, or shine a torch into the sky without fear of being shot at. This has not resulted in an immediate light-up in the town because the early-closing regulations are still in force and will probably remain for a long time yet so that the shops do not light up.

We thought we had heard the last of the bangs too but yesterday there were suddenly a number of terrific explosions which shook the house. Of course another thing that made our celebrations moderate was the fact that so many realised that we still have a big slice of war on our hands out East. We were thinking of Hugh who is flying his Barracuda somewhere out there now, and I'm afraid we were rather on the sober side. It has been going on for so long and we have for some time been expecting the end of the European war that there was no shock of surprise. Really it is very difficult to realise it now and to believe that probably our greatest danger is being run over by a bus. I wonder if we shall ever have to go to the shelter again. Grace said to Jo on VE Day plus one that we didn't seem to be as gay as we ought to be, and the little old lady of six said very seriously, 'Well, you see, Mummy, we still have to finish off the Japs.'

I'm sure you will forgive me if I cut this letter short as I shall have to get busy of course, but before closing I must mention that we had a visit on Monday from Miss Hunnybun. You remember the lady whose name you thought so funny. So did we – we had never heard it before – and this combined with the fact that she wrote such charming letters decided us that she must be American. Not so – she is very English. She is apparently a child psychologist by profession and a very nice person. She spent some months in the States recently and called on five hundred children, including twin boys in Cincinnati who had been giving a spot of trouble. She regretted that she had not had time to call on our three nuisances, but I gathered that she was there mainly to settle problems and you having raised the three children so nearly in your own image they naturally had a marvellous report from Mrs Clark of whom, by the way, Miss Hunnybun thinks quite a lot.

Janet Matthews to Grace and John Mathews

20 June 1945   925 Congress Avenue, Glendale, Ohio

The word came through two days ago that Cliff would be sailing on 22 June. We have been in a slight flurry trying to get things from the dry cleaners so we haven't had time to think about the fact that the ambassador is going home – I *wish* I could be there to see your faces when the young man steps off the boat! The girls are a little shaken up by having big brother leaving, but they know it won't be for long and we will do our best to keep them cheerful.

Cliff can give you all the news, so I won't attempt to give you any – the girls go to camp in Maine in a week, so only Bill, Mary, Terry and I will be left.

We will miss your big boy very much but it is a thrill to think that he will be with you.

Postscript by Bill Matthews

The 'man of few words' also wishes to send a message of greeting by way of your returning son whose visit with us we have enjoyed very much. He is a fine boy and we know how much you will enjoy having him home again – American accent and all.

John Mathews to Janet and Bill Matthews

8 July 1945   Hamilton, Hewarts Lane, Bognor Regis, Sussex

Cliff has been talking so much about you that you will see I have Aunt Janet so much on my mind that I even started off this letter with 'Aunt'.

Well, the great day arrived and we learned that he was coming into the London station at about 6 pm, and therefore I was able to get up there with Jo and Grace in time to meet him. We were waiting at the front of the train but I had an idea that he would be at the end, so I sneaked off by myself. Sure enough, I suddenly saw a head sticking way up above everyone else and after looking at him two or three times I decided that that worried-looking fellow must be Cliff. I waved and suddenly he discovered me and waved back and we forced our way towards one another and once again I was holding the hand of my favourite son. What a moment that was. All Cliff could say was, 'Gosh'. It was a terrific moment because all around us were people meeting their sons and daughters and husbands for the first time in years, and some of them were openly weeping. This made things all the more difficult, my own eyes became pretty watery, but everybody else in the family put up a good front so I had to pretend I had a bit of grit in my eye.

We had a real scramble to find the luggage and Cliff was getting pretty low about it because he thought it must be left behind in Liverpool. However, we eventually found it in the front of the train whereas we had been scrambling amongst the piles at the other end.

What a height the boy is. I think he was pretty scary when he first arrived and we had a job to get a smile out of him, but we let him have his head and now he has been with us nearly a week he is really settling down. Jo told him yesterday that he is a very nice boy and I think that is everyone's impression, and we want to say how thankful we are for the wonderful job you have done with this boy of ours: he is just what we should have liked him to become had we raised him ourselves over the last few years. He practised a piece of American kidding on me shortly after he arrived. I asked him how you took his leaving and he replied, 'Oh, I guess they were glad to get rid of me.' This set me back a bit and I said nothing in reply but later he showed me your letter to him, which came in record time, and I realised he was only kidding and he had a laugh on me. It is a good thing we are living here on the coast just now because we are having wonderful weather and he is able to get in plenty of his favourite sport. We have Cliff's cousin Betty sleeping in the air raid shelter this weekend, and she is a good swimmer too. We have spent the morning on the beach and have all been in the water, including Jo. We are getting some tea together to take with us and we hope to spend some time there this afternoon.

The school term at the County High School for boys ends on the eighteenth and I felt pretty tough when I had to bring up the question of school with Cliff but, as I told him, I thought it was best to get the matter settled and then he could just relax and enjoy life until he had to get down to studies. The headmaster asked Cliff to write down for him particulars of what he had been doing, but apparently this did not give the Doctor sufficient information to enable him to place Cliff. He wrote to me saying that he thought it best for Cliff to sit for the 4th Form's terminal examination.

Since writing the above, we have spent the afternoon on the beach and have finished supper, during which the subject of tomorrow's test at the school came up and Grace gave out that she thought it was unfair to push Cliff into a test so soon after his arrival home. I agreed it was tough, but suggested that it was better to get it over with rather than have it hanging over his head for the next two months. Cliff seemed to favour the idea of a correspondence course if he has to do anything but had apparently thought that his days at school were in any case nearly over, and the prospect of doing another twelve months seems to be anything but his idea of a good way to spend the time. I have to make up my mind before tomorrow morning so I will stop typing and concentrate on son Clifford or rather on his future. I will write again tomorrow evening and tell you the worst.

Well, here it is tomorrow evening, and Cliff's future education is not settled yet. Although he told me later that the master in the class in which he took the test was a very decent sort, the actual examination was quite beyond him because he had not been taking some of the subjects and had apparently not done any French for some time. As I told you, they cram these poor little blighters over here, and although Cliff is a year behind his contemporaries in most subjects he is probably several years ahead of them in physical well being, and as I count good health as one, if not the most important thing in a boy's upbringing, I am quite happy with the situation except that I feel terribly sorry for Cliff. I think I have persuaded him that I really am not in the least affected by what happened. When he came over to me at the depot, which is opposite the school, I took him off with me round the country on some calls I had to make. We lunched out together and then went to some estate agents to enquire about houses, soaked up some ice cream, which is very hard to get still, then went home to take tea with Mother. He is now sitting opposite me quite happily scribbling away a huge letter to Dave. He has already posted quite a long letter to you and then wrote to Sheila and Dinah.

Tomorrow Grace is taking him to Totton to his Grandma and Grandpa Mathews, and they are going to get a shock because we purposely have not told them of his return so that he could walk in and surprise them. I'd like to be there to see their faces, just as you would like to have seen us when we met Cliff. Then they are going over to see his cousin Barbara (the brain) and his uncle and aunt at the school at Michelmersh. They may stay the night so I shall be without my favourite son for a day and a night.

When I was taking him round with me after lunch he looked at me rather hopefully and said, 'You know, Dad, you could get a job anywhere in the States.' I laughed and replied, 'Suppose Uncle Sam refused to have me,' and he suggested that I could just pop over the border into Canada and come back again after a week. We have to smile when he is talking about the places he has been with you and he suddenly comes out with, 'Oh yes, that's another spot you'll have to see.' We have hardly stopped talking about his experiences since he arrived and he is becoming quite a talker. We had a letter from Sheila together with the one from you both, it was very nice to have a line from Bill and we appreciate very much your taking time out in the flurry to write such a very nice letter. Sheila made us laugh in hers because she said she thought that Grace and I would feel embarrassed with Cliff because of *our* accents. Why, when Cliff gets a bit excited every second word is 'guy', eg 'When the guy that was pitching sent down an inswinger to the guy that was batting, the guy thought it was a foul ball, changed his mind too late and the guy swung at it . . .'

Thank you very much for your cable re the girls' return. I don't know whether I told you but we heard through Miss Hunnybun that Mrs Clark had reported that they, the girls, were being questioned by reporters and their own friends as to when they were returning, and their inability to answer and give the whys and wherefores was embarrassing to them. Therefore, thinking it over, we decided that they might be getting depressed and rather sad at the idea of Cliff leaving them there, though how anyone could be sad and depressed in your household is beyond us. Cliff tells us that Miss Dinah lives from day to day and the future worries her not at all, but on the other hand Sheila is dead keen to see us once again, so maybe it is as well to get them over. Grace just aches to see them of course, but personally I feel that it would be pretty awful to get them over and then tell them that we cannot accommodate them and that they will have to live with their aunt and uncle near London. Therefore I feel that even if it means living in a caravan and tents it would be preferable to separating the family all over again. I can get a furnished house some time in October and in the meantime I may be able to purchase a caravan. I have asked their Uncle Les to go to the Cunard offices in London and find out what the position is regarding passage for them, and as soon as I have any news I will cable you. Cliff tells us that they are in camp at the moment and will be staying there for

174

some time. Sheila should be happy because we understand it is the one at which she can get in some riding and he says that she will be jumping this year. That should be very exciting for her and I would very much like to see her trying it. It was very very good of you to let them go.

I am writing this while waiting for a telephone call from Grace and Cliff to tell me what time they are arriving at Chichester from Michelmersh. They went off with Jo this morning and I regret to report that it has poured with rain all day. All right, you needn't laugh at our climate, he tells me it is as good as Ohio's. You see we are breaking down his resistance already.

Cliff has raised our hopes of seeing you both. He seems quite satisfied that you intend to come over. I do hope it is possible next spring or summer. We have questioned him closely about what you do in the evenings and weekends and we are cheered to know that our respective habits are somewhat similar, though of course I can't be sure about that because he failed to mention any of your bad habits, and you are either very very good or he is tremendously loyal to you. It must be the latter, I'm sure.

Well so long for the present and thank you for everything. We cannot replace you in Cliff's affections and we do not wish to do so, but we will do all we can to make him happy.

Janet Matthews to Grace and John Mathews

7 September 1945   Trelawny, Glendale, Ohio

Please forgive us for being so slow to thank you for your cable. We did appreciate it very much even if the long silence would not seem to indicate it. Somehow, the end of the war left us solemn and thankful but not at all in a mood to go about shouting and waving flags, which seemed to be the approved reaction.

This is a very sad evening. We are going to hate having the girls leave tomorrow. We know that we are terribly lucky – having the three nicest children in all England for so long – but I wish they were not so attractive and had a few irritating traits so that we could be a little pleased to see them go. What a thrill for you to have them all again. We will be thinking of you!

People keep popping in to say goodbye, so I won't attempt a letter. But I do want to thank you for lending us your children and to send our love to you and to ask you *please* not to forget to write as often as you can.

Postscript

The Mathews family reunited: Clifford, Sheila, Jo, Grace and Dinah on the beach at Aldwick, Sussex.

Postscript

The fond dream of sociologists, referred to in the introduction to these letters, in which, following the evacuation programme, 'a future generation of English will feel a lot warmer towards Americans and vice versa' certainly came true in the case of my own family. Three out of the four of us have married Americans.

However, the process of arriving at that happy state was not an easy one in the early period after the war ended. It was only when I went to America myself in 1959 that I began to understand how difficult it must have been for my sisters and brother to adjust to the austere conditions of life in post-war Britain after the comparative affluence to which they had become accustomed in the USA. The one small tin of sardines, the contents of which my mother served on toast as a special treat for supper the night the girls came home, would have been a negligible adjunct to their meals in Glendale, if eaten at all. The cramped housing conditions – the six of us spent the following summer in a caravan because we could not find permanent accommodation at that time – and the restricted educational and recreational facilities, not helped by the pervasive class consciousness of British society, to which they were particularly sensitive after their American experience, must have made those first years quite miserable in many ways.

Of course, we did have great fun at times as a reunited family, especially, as I remember it, round the dining table when my father and brother would engage in their favourite pastime of extended 'discussions', which often became quite heated. All very exciting for me, overwhelmed by the three beings from another world who had suddenly appeared as my older sisters and brother, an experience in reverse of the normal order. All very trying for my mother, who suddenly, after a relatively quiet war, had to cope with three children she must have felt she hardly knew, who were used to expressing their views without reserve and to receiving on most occasions a reasoned and sympathetic response. 'You'll do it because I say so' did not go unchallenged.

Dinah was not submissive by temperament. I recall in the early days after her return, when we were both attending the same primary school, seeing an enormous pile of bodies being disentangled by a teacher after a playground fight. Second from bottom in the pile was Dinah, who had thrown herself in to protect someone she thought was being unjustly attacked. Her dress was torn and her hair pulled in every direction, but her eyes were twinkling and she was having a hard time keeping a straight face under the admonitions of the teacher. I think it was her ability to detach herself a little from the bizarre world into which she had been plunged and above all to find relief in wonderfully infectious laughter which carried her through. She also had an outlet in dancing and music, both of which she loved, and in reading, although this brought her into conflict with our mother who would protest that she 'always has her head in a book when I want her to do something'.

So none of us was surprised when soon after taking her 'O' Level exams in England she accepted Janet and Bill Matthews's offer to see her through secretarial college in the States if she wanted to return there. She met and married her husband John, a psychiatrist, while she was working at Columbia University, and he chose to study in England during his year as a Fulbright scholar. The first of their three children was born in London. Sadly, John died of cancer. Dinah lives now in their New York home and works for a doctor nearby.

Cliff's education during the year he spent at Portsmouth Technical College after returning home probably owed more to the cinemas and swimming pool than to the classroom. After his eighteenth birthday he was drafted into the army, proceeded to officer training, during which time he was known as 'The Yank', and to national service in the Middle East, where he further developed his taste for travel. Back in Sussex he made a brave attempt to start farming the hard way as a labourer in the fields, but it soon became evident that without capital this was going to lead no further than a lifetime topping and tailing mangel wurzels, and he returned to the States. He joined Thomas Cook's in New York, and he met his American wife there. They moved to Florida where their daughter was born and Cliff set up his own travel business, Chartwell. Now he has retired early so that he can travel more himself. He still plays a very vigorous game of tennis and paints and sketches, having inherited a talent for drawing from my father.

Sheila's undoubted social skills made it possible for her to be more completely reabsorbed into the English way of life for some years. She married a Scottish doctor and had five children, two of whom have studied in the USA. She herself has taken a degree in American Studies since her family grew up. Now a widow, she returns to visit Aunt Janet regularly and keeps in touch with all the families in the States including the Strohmengers.

Janet and Bill did visit the One Ts in England before too many years had passed after the war and, happily, the two couples got on as well together in person as they had done through their letters. My parents had a tremendously exciting and exhausting visit to the States to see all the places the children had enjoyed and my mother kept up her visits to her children over there into her eighty-seventh year. Janet Matthews, though now a widow, continues to divide her time between her homes in Florida and Glendale, and to take a very active interest in the village and her family.

The Two Ts side of the equation has remained more numerous on the American side of the ocean, but 'B' and his wife Mary spent a good deal of time in Europe, where 'B' continued the families' tradition of promoting greater international understanding by working for an organisation which brings children of many different nationalities together in summer villages. They lived in Newcastle-upon-Tyne, England, until 'B' died in 1989. Harry runs the family business in Ohio. Don is Professor of Political Science in Seattle and a frequent visitor to England.

Warren Strohmenger returned to re-establish his medical practice in Ohio after the war, but never threw off the shadow of his experience at Iwo Jima, and Jean is now a widow. Gloria is married and her son has visited Sheila's family in England.

My father died in 1958 leaving a gap in all our lives and I felt that the time had come to go and see for myself what I had heard so much about from the others, and even to go a little further. After visiting the East Coast I went on to California, where I met my husband, an American architect. We lived in San Francisco for five years during which time our son was born. We have moved back and forth across the Atlantic but our base has been in England since 1969 and I am lucky enough to work in what is, not surprisingly, the area of my greatest interest, international relations, at the Royal Institute of International Affairs in London. Under our influence, some of my husband's family, although firmly rooted in the American mid-West, have been tempted to leave the dog-days of a Missouri summer and sample the bracing air of an English August.

My family's wartime experience saved us from what could have been the narrow provincialism of life in a small Hampshire village. Now we enjoy an uneasy disequilibrium poised between two cultures. I think we do, however, enjoy the disequilibrium. My father hoped the evacuation scheme would help to promote better transatlantic relations. Within our family it certainly has and perhaps we have managed to help spread this a little more widely. In the early days we undoubtedly annoyed people in Britain by praising American virtues too extravagantly. Now we take a more balanced view of the good and bad in both countries.

One American virtue we can never overrate is their unhesitating generosity, though the British still sometimes regard it as a form of naïvety. These letters show what a powerful force it was in the grim days of the last war and I hope they will help to prevent it ever being forgotten.